D1207266

The Lakota Way of
Strength and Courage

Other Books by Joseph M. Marshall III

Nonfiction

Returning to the Lakota Way: Ancient Values for the Modern World (2012)

To You We Shall Return: Lessons About Our Planet from the Lakota

The Power of Four: Leadership Lesson of Crazy Horse

Keep Going: The Art of Perseverance

The Day the World Ended at Little Bighorn: A Lakota History

Walking with Grandfather: The Wisdom of Lakota Elders

The Journey of Crazy Horse: A Lakota History

The Lakota Way: Stories and Lessons for Living

The Dance House: Stories from Rosebud

On Behalf of the Wolf and the First Peoples

Fiction

The Long Knives Are Crying

Hundred in the Hand

Winter of the Holy Iron

How Not to Catch Fish: And Other Adventures of Iktomi (children's)

Audio

To You We Shall Return: Lessons About Our Planet from the Lakota

Quiet Thunder: The Wisdom of Crazy Horse

Stories from the Lakota Way

The Lakota Way of Strength and Courage

Lessons in Resilience from the Bow and Arrow

Joseph M. Marshall III

SOUNDS TRUE
Boulder, Colorado

Sounds True, Inc.
Boulder, CO 80306

Cover and book design by Rachael Murray

Printed in Canada

Library of Congress Cataloging-in-Publication Data

Marshall, Joseph, 1945–
  The Lakota way of strength and courage : lessons in resilience from the bow and arrow / Joseph M. Marshall III.
      p. cm.
  1. Teton Indians—History. 2. Teton philosophy. 3. Teton Indians—Social life and customs. I. Title.
  E99.T34.M36 2012
  978.004'975244—dc23
                                        2011028292

eBook ISBN 978-1-60407-747-6

10 9 8 7 6 5 4 3 2 1

For Connie

Contents

Child of the Moon, Child of the Sun

THERE WAS A TIME when Lakota boys looked at a new bow and arrows the way any modern teenager gazes at an iPod, a cell phone, or the latest version of a video game—longingly and lovingly. There was one basic difference, however. Lakota boys eventually learned how to make their own bows and arrows and learned the life lessons associated with them.

Bows and arrows have been around for thousands of years and, as weapons for hunting and warfare, were critical to the survival of cultures all over the world. They were frequently and literally the difference between starvation and plenty and very often between life and death.

Although I heard about the bow (*itazipa*) and the arrow (*wahinkpe*) in stories told by both of my maternal grandparents, I never actually saw the real thing until my grandfather made a set in 1950. The bow was of ash wood, and the arrows were thin chokecherry stalks. Like countless Lakota boys before me, I was immediately drawn to them. The feeling was somewhat like meeting an old friend. More than likely, I felt an inherent cultural connection with them. My lifelong fascination began the moment my grandfather placed the arrows, one at a time, on the bowstring and shot them into the air. As I watched those feathered shafts arc gracefully through the sky, I knew they would be part of my life for as long as I lived.

When I asked where the bow came from, it was my grandmother who replied.

"From the moon," she said.

She explained that the moon was a woman, and it was she who gave us Lakota the bow. I accepted what she said without question. Several evenings later, she showed me the sliver of a new moon hanging in the sky. The thin, silver crescent looked exactly like my grandfather's bow when he drew it back to shoot an arrow.

According to my grandfather, someone in the distant past saw that same sliver of a new moon and related it to the function of a bow. A bow works by reacting to being drawn, or bent, when the archer pulls back on the string. When the string is released, the reflexive action launches the arrow. Anyone who is familiar with how a bow works, and especially anyone who has constructed primitive bows, knows that the bow must be designed to withstand the stress of being drawn or bent. Bad design or poor craftsmanship will cause one or both of the limbs to work improperly or even break under stress.

If nothing else, a primitive Lakota bow is the epitome of simplicity. When strung—that is, when the string is attached to both tips—it resembles a narrow capital *D*. It is widest in the middle, the point where the archer holds it. The length from below this handle to the tip is the bottom limb, or wing. Above the handle is the top limb. In order for the bow to function smoothly time after time, both limbs have to bend uniformly. In other words, the stress has to be equal on both limbs.

The thinnest sliver of a new moon also is widest in the middle and gradually tapers to both ends. As my grandfather said, some archer in the distant past realized that he (or she)

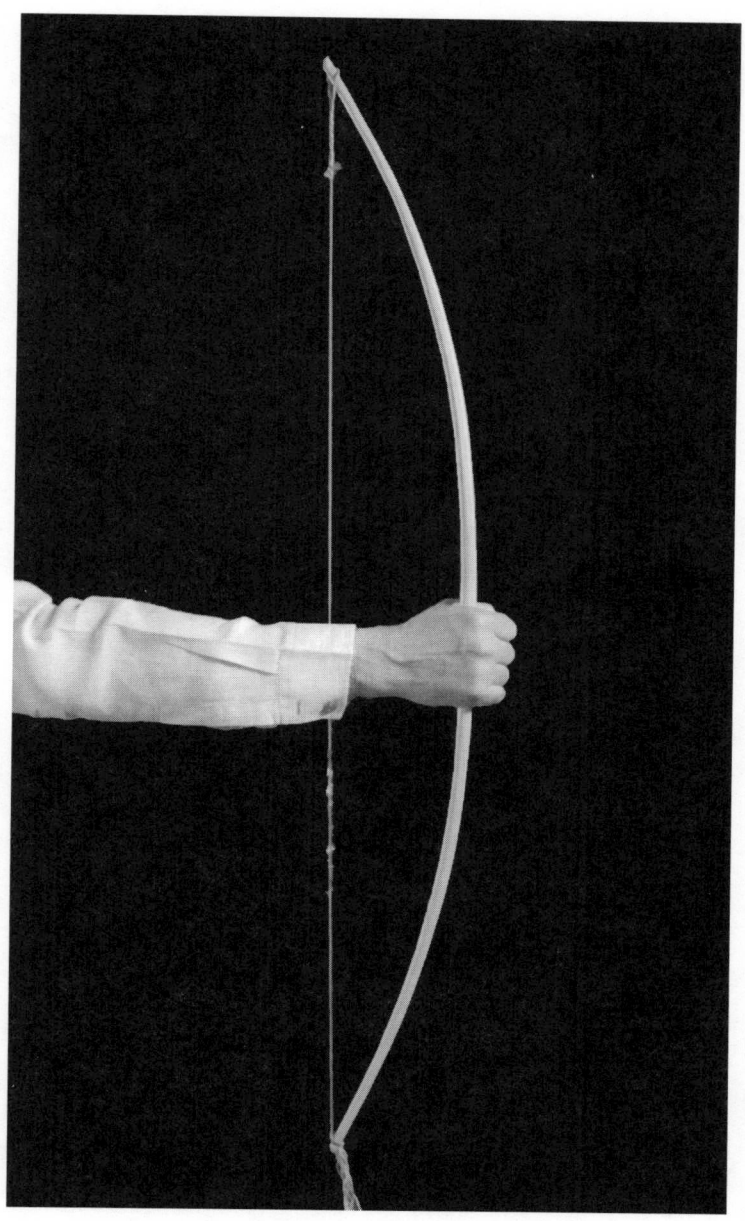

Lakota ashwood bow with sinew string

was looking at a design wherein the limbs of a bow would flex, or bend, evenly. Therefore, practically, as well as spiritually, the moon did give us the bow.

Sooner or later, I asked the next obvious question: if the bow came from the moon, where did the arrow come from?

"From the sun," was my grandfather's reply.

I already knew that the sun was considered a man, so I deduced—correctly, as it turned out—that the arrow must be male. One late afternoon, when the sun's rays were shafts of light descending through a broken bank of clouds, my grandfather pointed to them. Those were the arrows of the sun. While the bow was a graceful curve, the arrow was absolutely as straight as straight could be.

Neither the moon nor the sun told us what sort of material the bow and arrow were to be made of. However, given that my Lakota ancestors harvested from the natural environment everything they used, wore, lived in, and ate, they knew the characteristics of every kind of raw material. Hardwoods were used for bows because they were more flexible than softwoods, and both soft- and hardwood stalks were used for arrows.

In pre-reservation days, bows and arrows were absolute necessities for the Lakota hunter/warrior. He used that weapon set to procure the resources needed for food, shelter, and clothing, as well as to defend family, home, and community against enemies. Around the age of twelve, every boy began to learn to craft them. It was a skill refined and polished year after year. There were usually a few who were much more skilled than others. Nevertheless, every man in the village was a bow maker and arrow smith.

During the first years on the reservations, bows and arrows were still being made and used for hunting. Some were made to sell to whites, and several white collectors had been able to acquire some prior to the reservation era. There were still many

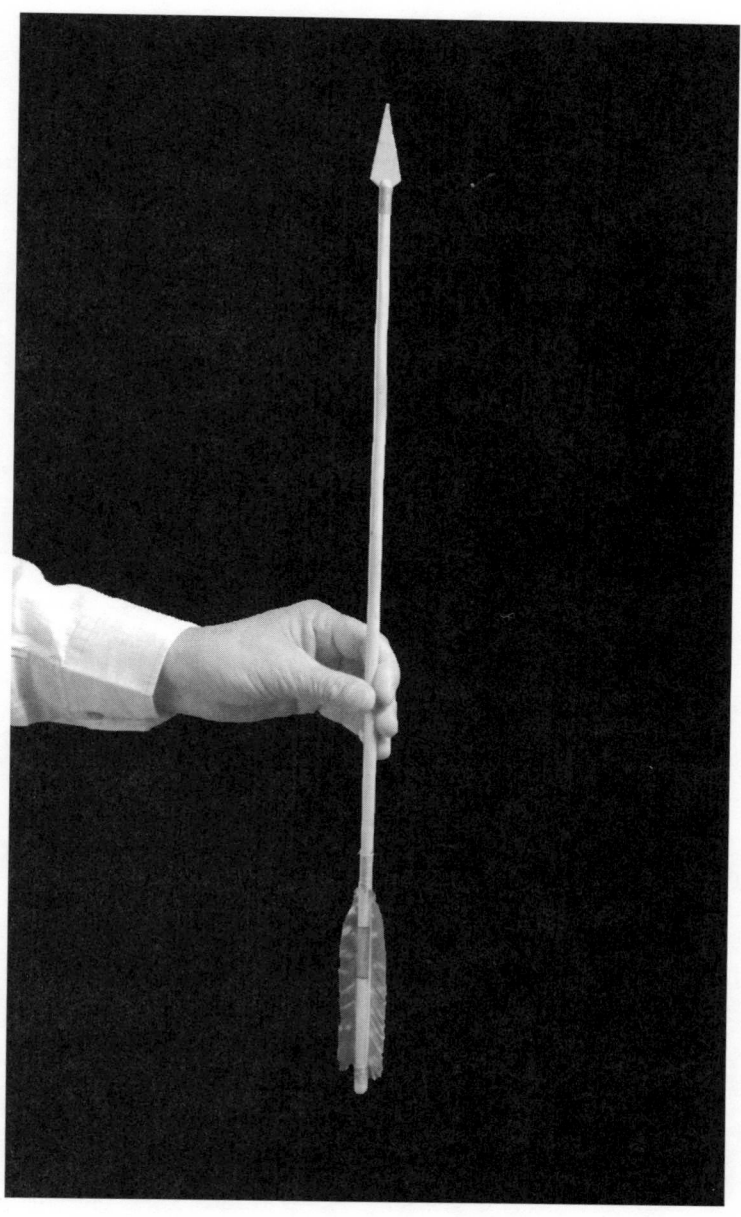

Lakota arrow with turkey feathers and iron point

men of my grandparents' generation, like my grandfather, who had the knowledge and skills to make bows and arrows. My father had a basic knowledge, but as far as I know, he never made or used them. Technically speaking, the Lakota primitive bow and arrow have not been lost to history, but they have only barely survived.

Various cultures look at the bow and arrow as more than weapons, as more than the physical objects they are. That was certainly true among my ancestors. Lakota archers, who individually crafted their own bows and arrows, looked at the *before* and *after*. They saw the bow and the arrow as a process. And in that process they found the connections to, and associations with, life. Over time, there emerged protocols and philosophies regarding the crafting and use of bows and arrows.

For example, when an oak, ash, or chokecherry tree was cut to make a bow, the bottom end of the tree was always marked. Therefore, the archer knew which end of the finished bow would be the bottom and which would be the top.

A single string notch was carved into the top tip, and two notches were carved into the bottom tip, one on each side. A bow was kept unstrung, the string detached from the top limb notch, until there was a reason to use it. Then the archer would string the bow and, for a moment, perhaps a heartbeat, touch the bottom of his bow to the earth. There was a simple but profound reason for that ritual. For that heartbeat in time, the bow was realigned with the earth to connect it to the life-giving force it had known when it was a living tree.

There were similar rituals for the arrow. Like the bow wood, a stalk selected to be an arrow was marked at the bottom or root end when cut. That end, the thickest part of the shaft, was the nock end, the end that was notched (usually in a vee) so that the finished arrow could be placed on the string. When an archer was about to shoot his first arrow, he placed, or nocked, the arrow on the string. Then he lifted his bow to point the arrow vertically, in order to acknowledge the arrow's configuration when it was a living stalk. If the archer was on foot, as opposed to mounted on a horse, he touched the nock end of the arrow to the ground before he placed it on the string.

The reason for both the bow and arrow rituals was simple: the archer, who was also the craftsman, demonstrated respect for the objects, which were once living things, by briefly reconnecting or realigning them with the life force of Grandmother Earth.

Because of simple yet profound philosophies such as these, the basis for this book is the primitive version of the Lakota bow and arrow, used by my ancestors for hundreds of years before the Lakota people were forced to live on reservations. There were two basic kinds of bows and arrows: those used for hunting and those used for warfare. There were also the versions used before my ancestors acquired the horse, and those adapted or redesigned after the horse came. Whatever their historical origin, Lakota primitive bows and arrows were and are reflections of life, of the process that occurs from birth to death.

When, as a boy, I watched my grandfather shoot his bow, and when he made a bow and arrows for me and put them in my hand, little did I know my association with them would be lifelong. Over the years, I have owned and used many bows. But the strongest sense of connection I feel is with the bows and arrows I make, because they reach across time. My skill and the hours of labor I spend making those bows and arrows put me in the company of all the Lakota craftsmen and archers before me who did the same. It is a circle, starting with them and ending with me. The knowledge and ability to make a bow and an arrow came from them. And, like my ancestors, I have learned lessons from those simple objects.

The lessons were not simple, but were many and profound. I suspect there are more yet to come. A few have had a lasting impact on me, as they have to do with issues that all of us encounter at some point in our lives, frequently more than once. For this book, I have selected five lessons:

- Transformation
- Simplicity
- Purpose
- Strength
- Resiliency

These five are not all there is to life, but they are the lessons from the bow and arrow that are most consistent for me. Of the five, one is a process, and the others are characteristics. All can be related directly to the art of making primitive bows and arrows, and to most things in life.

1

Transformation

A Bag of Stones

Long ago, before the coming of horses, the people were strong and prosperous. Their villages were many across the wide prairie lands west of the Muddy River. Their strength came from a well-ordered society with rules of conduct for both men and women. Men were the hunters and warriors, the providers and protectors. Women were the center of the family, the first teachers of the children. Children were taught early that everything and everyone had a place and a purpose. Elders were revered as the source of knowledge and wisdom. Everyone treated elders with courtesy and respect.

However, in one village, which pitched its lodges along the Bad River, there was one boy who did not heed all the lessons he had learned. His name was White Wing. He was a tall, good-looking boy on the verge of young manhood, the only child of Bear Eyes and Walks Far Woman. Like all Lakota parents, they had doted on the boy, teaching him to be a good and compassionate person. But perhaps because he was taller and stronger than other boys his age, he was somewhat vain. Things that other boys struggled to learn and master had come easily to White Wing. More and more, he would walk through the village, his head held high, knowing that he was the center of attention.

White Wing's growing arrogance was cause for concern because his father was the leader of the warriors and head of the Red Hand Warrior's Society of men who had been wounded in battle. Bear Eyes was a fair and humble man, and most people were puzzled that any son of his could tend toward vanity and arrogance. People talked about White Wing in whispers behind their hands, wondering what Bear Eyes would do about his son.

Bear Eyes and Walks Far Woman had already decided what to do about their son. One fine morning, the leader of warriors paid a visit to an old man, a widower and the village's only medicine man. Grasshopper was the old man's name. Stories circulated in many villages about the mysterious, mostly blind medicine man. Much of it was gossip, but everyone knew that no one was wiser, shrewder, or trickier than old Grasshopper.

A few days after the leader's visit, Bear Eyes took his son to the lodge of the old medicine man. He told White Wing that Grasshopper had need of his help. Near a shallow, chalky stream to the south were special river stones that the old medicine man wanted to gather so that he could use them in a sweat lodge ceremony. As everyone knew, stones were heated in a large fire pit and placed into the center pit of the half-dome sweat lodge. Then a medicine man poured water to create steam for purification for the participants. White Wing had taken part in many sweats.

White Wing knew that Grasshopper's request was the same as being told what to do. He did not want to anger

his father by refusing, so he agreed to help the old man
gather the stones and bring them back to the village.

As the following dawn broke over the eastern horizon,
Grasshopper and White Wing were on their way.
Grasshopper had no weapons; he used only a walking stick
and carried an elk hide, a water flask, a bag full of things
the boy could not see, and a rolled-up bag made of tanned
elk skin for carrying the stones. White Wing had his own
water flask, a food bag, a bow and a quiver of arrows, a
lance, and a deer-hide blanket.

They traveled slowly, owing to the old man's age
and bad eyesight. The boy stifled his impatience. The
first evening, he gathered wood, built a fire, and shared
his *wasna*—a mixture of dried bison meat and pounded
chokecherries mixed with tallow, an oil rendered from
fat—with his companion.

"It would be good to have fresh meat," the old man said,
as the sun was going down and the fire dying out. "Perhaps
my grandson can shoot a fat grouse or two for us tomorrow.
Just before sunrise is the best time to hunt for them."

Dutifully, though somewhat irritated, White Wing
arose before dawn and went to a nearby plateau. There
he waited until the male prairie grouse began dancing,
stomping the ground, and drumming their wings. The boy
crawled through the grass until he was close enough for a
shot, and he successfully took two birds.

Grasshopper noisily enjoyed the meal of roast grouse,
abruptly gathered his things, and struck out on the trail.
For a mostly blind old man, he seemed to know where
he was going. White Wing hurriedly put out the fire,
gathered his own things, and followed the old man.

After three more days of walking, they descended
into a broad valley and made camp near the confluence

of two rivers. One river was the shallow, chalky stream. Grasshopper indicated that the stones he needed could be found upriver, west of where the rivers met.

"I will wait here," he told the boy. "Tomorrow you will gather the stones. I need four, round like the moon, and each must be bigger than the one before it. Put them in this." He tossed the elk-hide bag to White Wing.

"There is still daylight," the boy protested. "I will go and get those stones now."

"No," the old man replied. "I am hungry for fish. There are large blackfish with the long whiskers in that river. Spear a big one for us."

Not bothering to hide his irritation with the old man, the boy stomped away with his lance. Just before sundown, he returned with a large, whiskered blackfish (catfish). With grumbles of protest, he butchered the fish, skewered it on green stalks, and hung it over the fire. The old man seemed not to pay any attention to the boy's discomfort. Instead, he sat with his eyes closed, singing a song to the spirits.

As a matter of fact, the old man did not speak to the boy for the entire evening, except to thank him for spearing the fish and cooking it. As darkness fell, he cleared a place to sleep and curled up under his elk hide.

White Wing sat alone, watching the stars come out and listening to owls, barking coyotes, the occasional bellow of a bison bull, and the melodious song of wolves. He had never been far from home alone. He pulled his weapons close. His father had mentioned that this area was known for bears—the large humped bears that were much bigger than a grown man. He might as well be alone, he thought. The old man would be no help if a bear appeared. The boy hurriedly gathered

more firewood, deciding to keep the fire burning
through the night.

The next morning, he awoke to hear the medicine
man singing a sunrise song. Later, they finished what was
left of the fish.

"I will wait here while you gather the stones. When you
return with them, we will start for home," Grasshopper
told the boy.

Mumbling under his breath, the boy snatched up
the elk-hide bag and headed for the chalky river.
Before long, he found the bend in the river the old
medicine man described, and on the old part of the
riverbed were countless stones. Grasshopper's descriptions
of the stones he wanted were puzzling, but finding
that kind of stones was not hard. Soon the boy had
picked out the four stones and headed back for camp.

Grasshopper opened the bag and looked briefly at the
stones. "Good," he said. "Now we go home. But we will
go west. There is a narrow valley with a creek, and the
bottomland is thick with sweet grass. I want to gather as
much as we can carry."

White Wing sighed. He was anxious to go home,
but not the long way. As they gathered their things and
prepared to break camp, he considered taking a more
direct route back to their village. But he knew his father
would be angry if he arrived home without the old man.
So the tall, handsome boy on the verge of manhood
trudged along, pouting silently, and wondering what old
people were good for.

On the second day, the old man once again spoke his
yearning for fresh meat, this time deer. Half-heartedly
White Wing probed a long, narrow gully for almost half
a day. He managed to frighten a deer from its bed, but

it bounded away and was quickly out of bow range. At least he had tried, he told himself. When he returned to camp, he found the old man roasting two rabbits over the fire.

"They must be blind like me," the old man joked. "They got caught in some snares I set by that creek." He said nothing about the fact that the boy had returned empty-handed.

The boy ate sullenly, hoping that the next two or three days would pass quickly. By the afternoon of the next day, he could contain his frustration and impatience no longer. In spite of the weight of the bag of stones, he walked faster and faster, knowing the old man could not keep up. Nothing wrong with a little fun, he thought, wondering what the medicine man would do when he suddenly realized he was alone.

From the top of a low hill, White Wing stopped and looked back. The old man was plodding along, picking his way with his walking stick. The boy decided to run to the next hill. Enjoying his new game of teasing the old man, he reached the hill and began to trot down the slope, intending to have a drink from the creek. He did not see the bear until he nearly ran into it.

The animal was already standing on its back legs. It was a deep brown in color and looked to be twice as tall as a grown man. White Wing heard a soft, inquisitive "woof," dropped the bag of stones, and stood rooted to the ground for a few heavy heartbeats.

White Wing's bow was in its case, unstrung, the lance all but forgotten. Never in his young life had he known such a moment. The boy and the bear stared at one another. In the next heartbeat, White Wing was sprinting as fast as he could toward a tall cottonwood tree. Behind him, he heard the bear's grunts and knew that it was gaining on him with every step.

How the boy made it to the first low branch would always be a mystery to him. A swipe from the bear's enormous front paw sliced into the back of his leg and tore off his moccasin. Then he heard the animal's claws scratching at the bark of the tree. Out of its cavernous chest came a bellowing roar.

Driven by a fear he had never known, White Wing grabbed for the higher branches, pulling himself up as fast as he could. From below, he heard the bear grunting with its efforts to climb. The boy did not notice that the bow and quiver of arrows had slipped off his shoulder. Panting heavily, he kept climbing until he could go no higher. On the ground, the bear was now circling the tree.

White Wing, weak with relief and shaking, watched the bear. He was prepared to spend the day in the tree, but then he thought of the old man, probably still walking toward the creek unaware of the angry bear. Even if he was aware, he could not see beyond the length of his arm, nor could he hope to outrun the bear.

To White Wing's dismay, the bear suddenly turned its attention away from the tree. Looking down the narrow little valley, the boy saw Grasshopper feeling his way along with his walking stick. At the base of the tree, the bear rose up on its back legs, dropped down, and trotted toward the old man. The boy put his head down; he could not watch. It was not difficult to imagine what would happen when the huge bear got hold of the defenseless old man.

White Wing sat in the tree waiting to hear the bear tear the medicine man apart. He had never seen a bear attack anything, animal or man, but he had heard stories from hunters. One had seen a bear chase and catch a young elk cow.

Suddenly, he realized that everything was silent. No birds were calling. Even the breeze had stopped. Through the branches of the trees, he could see the bear and the old medicine man facing each other. Grasshopper reached into his bag, took something out, and waved it at the bear. The bear reacted strangely. After a moment, it backed away. After several more moments, it retreated, crossed the creek, and loped across a clearing into a grove of trees. From his vantage point in the top of the cottonwood tree, White Wing saw the bear trot over a hill and disappear.

White Bear scrambled down from the tree, more than a little ashamed of himself for not being able to do anything to help the old man.

"Grandfather," he called out, after reaching the old man. "You are not hurt. The bear did not attack you."

The old man nodded and smiled. "This is a good day," he said.

"What did you do?" the boy wanted to know.

"I gave that bear something to think about," the old man replied. "Do you have the bag of stones?"

"No, Grandfather," the boy admitted. "I dropped them. And my bow and lance."

"Let us find your things and the stones. Then we can build a fire and have something to eat."

"But the bear," White Wing fretted. "It might come back."

"No," the old man replied, smiling. "I think he will stay away from us."

As it turned out, they were not far from the little valley where the sweet grass grew. A breeze carried its sweet

scent. Grasshopper insisted on eating, and soon there was
a fire. White Wing gathered a large pile of firewood, not
entirely convinced the bear would stay away, especially
during the night.

The old man made tea by heating a handful of small
stones in the fire. He placed the hot stones into the
water in his bison-horn cup and added dried mint leaves.
After they finished the last of their dried bison meat,
Grasshopper was silent and seemed to be staring off to a
place only he could see. White Wing waited, instinctively
knowing that something was about to happen. He did not
have to wait long.

"Show me the stones in your bag," the old man said.

White Wing opened the bag and took out the stones.

"Put them in a straight line," Grasshopper instructed.
"First the small one, then the next biggest ones. The largest
one should be last."

Again, the boy did as he was instructed. Four stones sat
in a straight line, smallest to largest.

The old man cleared his throat. "I am glad you
picked nice round stones," he said. "Because life is like
that. Life is a circle, like all of these stones. Look at the
sun. It is round, a circle, and so is the moon. Drop a
stone in a pond, and you see circles grow. The seasons
go in a circle: winter, spring, summer, and autumn, over
and over. When we pray, we start by facing west, where
the Great Powers live; then we turn north, then east,
then south. We show our respect to all our relatives by
moving in a circle."

The boy listened. He knew these things because all
elders talked this way.

"Pick up the smallest stone," the old man said.

White Wing did as he was asked.

"Even the life each of us lives is a circle," Grasshopper went on. "First we are like the stone in your hand—small, because as babies we know nothing and must depend on our family for everything." He pointed to the next stone, a little larger than the first. The boy picked it up and put down the other.

"In our childhood, the next stone, we learn the most because everything we learn is new to us. Our parents and grandparents and all the people in the village teach us how to behave, what our place is, how to do the things to make our lives comfortable and safe. This is where you are."

He pointed to the next stone, again slightly larger than the previous one.

"That is when we have grown up. Our bodies have reached the size we will be. As adults, we begin to build knowledge, to take our place in the village, to do the kinds of things we need to for families. We raise our own families. We hunt, and we fight when we need to. This is where your mother and father are. Now, pick up the last stone."

White Wing picked up the fourth stone.

"Pick up the first three with your other hand," the medicine man said.

White Wing did as he was told.

"The fourth stone is heavier than the others together," Grasshopper asserted.

The boy was astonished. It was so.

"The fourth stone is the final part of our lives, when we are preparing to finish the circle of our lives. Our bodies grow weaker, but we have done and learned much. Like that stone, we are heavy with knowledge, and we grow wise."

"This is where you are, Grandfather," the boy said timidly.

"Yes. I am in the final part of my life. I cannot do the things I did as a younger man, but I have learned things. Now it is my responsibility to give back the gift life has given me."

"What is that, Grandfather?" the boy wanted to know.

"Wisdom. It is why your mother and father talked to me about you. They want you to learn the right things so that you can be a good man. So in our little journey together I have been watching and thinking. I have decided what it is that you should learn."

"I am listening, Grandfather," White Wing whispered, afraid of what he was about to hear.

"Silence is difficult to ignore," the old man said.

The boy nodded politely, though he was confused. He had no idea what it meant. Moments passed, and the old man spoke again.

"You are wondering why the bear did not attack me."

"Yes, Grandfather," the boy admitted.

The old man smiled and reached into his bag and pulled out a wooden vial. Pulling off the plug, he held the open vial out to the boy. Immediately, the sharp, pungent odor of skunk assaulted the boy's nose. He recoiled.

Putting the vial away, the old man chuckled. "I could not see that bear clearly," he said, "but I think it was an older one, perhaps like me. A bear's nose can smell at great distances. It can smell things under rocks and even roots in the ground. A skunk's spray can be very painful to a bear's nose, and this one probably had a fight with a skunk at one time. He has never forgotten, which is fortunate for me. If it had been a young bear that knew nothing about skunks, the outcome would have been different. My grandfather taught me to carry a little vial of skunk oil, just for bears."

Days later, their journey was complete. The old medicine man and the boy arrived home with bundles of sweet grass and a bag of stones. Grasshopper told the boy to keep the stones as a reminder of their journey. Later that autumn he taught the boy how to trap a skunk and extract the oil from the animal's scent glands so that he could carry his own vial of skunk oil.

Now and then, White Wing pondered what the old man had said. "Silence is difficult to ignore." He did notice that when the breeze stopped or a wind calmed, people had a tendency to look around at the landscape and into the sky. Sometimes when White Wing found himself alone on a river bottom or out on the open prairie, there were moments when utter silence prevailed. No wind, no bird calls, no elk whistling, nothing. Only utter, profound silence. Such moments always made him pause.

But it was not until the old medicine man died the following spring that he learned the meaning of the old man's words.

People came from many villages for the old man's funeral. They feasted in his honor and talked of his life. An old, old man spoke the day the medicine man was laid to rest on his burial scaffold on a hillside. White Wing was surprised to learn that as a young man Grasshopper had been known as High Whirlwind. In the prime of his life, he had been a stalwart warrior, one who had won many honors and the respect of everyone who knew him. It was a part of his life that the thin, nearly blind old man had never spoken of.

Silence is difficult to ignore.

White Wing understood what it meant. He visited the old man's burial scaffold as often as he could over the years.

And over the years he grew into the quiet, compassionate man his mother and father hoped he would.

THE CONVERSATIONS OF OLD MEN

In the 1950s, I once overheard several old Lakota men on the Rosebud Sioux Indian Reservation talking about the past. Their generation often did, since their grandparents, born in the 1860s, were the last to live the nomadic life that preceded the U.S. government's establishment of the reservation in 1881. Such conversations frequently compared the present to the past. Understandably, there was always a certain amount of nostalgia and regret.

This particular conversation took place on a Sunday afternoon following an Episcopal church service. The church was in a rural area along a highway, six miles from the nearest town, in the northern part of the reservation. The all-Lakota congregation had gathered for a picnic near a log house not far from the frame church. As I recall, everything was quite formal and subdued until the white Episcopalian priest had finished his meal and left. Then all manner of activity and conversations broke out. In a nearby field, a group of teenage boys and young men played a game akin to lacrosse. Women gathered in their own groups, and younger children were everywhere. I stayed near my grandfather and a group of old men who chose to sit in the shade of a cottonwood tree and watch what was going on around them.

One of the men commented that, in the old days, there were only horses instead of cars and buffalo-hide lodges instead of log houses. Someone mentioned that some of the current generation of Lakota children were as fluent in "speaking white man" (meaning English) as they were in Lakota. All the old men agreed that speaking white man was a survival mechanism, given that "things had changed" for us; they meant that white people were in control, and knowing their language was necessary.

A few moments later, another of the grandfathers lamented that the loss of the ability to speak Lakota would mean the loss of Lakota customs and traditions, all the things that made us who and what we were as a people. Nearly thirty years later, I realized that those old men were talking about nothing less than how a culture—in this case, the Lakota culture—is transformed by circumstances and events outside its control.

I know now that *cultural memory* is the mechanism by which all aspects of culture, everything that identifies a group of people as a distinct society or nation—language, customs, traditions, history, myths, legends, and spiritual beliefs—are passed from one generation to the next. I also know that the transformation those old men were in such a quandary over affected Lakota cultural memory.

One of those old men said the changes that had happened to the Lakota people between the 1850s and the 1950s were like a circle of light, cast by the flames of a torch or the beam of a flashlight, moving in the darkness. All the old men, my maternal grandfather among them, agreed with the analogy. They agreed that because of two to three generations of difficult changes, cultural memory was hanging on to the trailing edge of that circle of light. Once that light moved on, many things would be left in the darkness.

One of those old men took that analogy a step further, a viewpoint that I have never forgotten. He used the *stone arrowhead* as a prime example of how change can and does transform us and the things, beliefs, and institutions attendant to being who we are.

Projectile points, including arrow points, have been part of the human arsenal of weaponry for tens (perhaps hundreds) of thousands of years—for so long, in fact, that the skills for making projectile points were carefully and methodically passed from one generation of craftsmen to the next. The skills for making stone arrowheads involved knowing which type of stone was suitable for the task, the grain patterns in such stone, how to make and use appropriate stone-carving tools, how to fracture or flake the stone to produce flakes, and the methods of percussion and pressure flaking.

For the Lakota, the craft of making stone arrowheads came to a sudden end around 1840, after cast iron became consistently available to them and other indigenous peoples of the northern plains. Iron came in the form of knives, tools, utensils, and cookware such as skillets and pots. Such items were obtained primarily through trade with Euro-Americans. Almost immediately came the realization that iron could be used in the crafting of traditional Lakota weapons—more precisely, the lance point and arrowhead. It was an understandable transition, because iron was more durable than stone. Furthermore, with the right tools, it was possible to make iron arrowheads in less time than it took to craft a stone point.

In a few years, most Lakota hunter/warriors had switched completely to using iron for lance and arrow points, and for knife blades as well. By 1865, there was enough iron available that boys no longer needed to learn to craft stone points. By the mid-1870s, two generations of Lakota males had not learned the skills for making stone points. The knowledge still existed in those older hunter/warriors who had learned and practiced those ancient skills as young men. By the early 1900s, much of the knowledge of that art had died with the last of those old, pre-reservation Lakota men.

The old man who made the analogy had learned from his father the mostly forgotten art of making stone arrowheads. He, the son, continued to make stone points in order to say that the skill had not died out completely, and he offered to teach anyone who wanted to learn. Sadly, there were not many who took him up on the offer. The establishment of reservations and a drastic change in Lakota lifestyle relegated stone arrowheads and the skills for making them to the hazy edge of cultural awareness. Inevitably, they were lost to the darkness beyond the light of that awareness.

Cultures, like individuals, more often than not are transformed by changes in circumstance. That transformation can mean the culture will evolve into something better or stronger, or it can be the opposite. I think those old men I listened to that day in the 1950s were not convinced their people were undergoing a good transformation. They were not certain that the Lakota would become a stronger or better people as a consequence of interaction with Euro-Americans. And they were concerned because that interaction was not simple. Lakota people were living and functioning under the control of white people (the U.S. government). Their basic and most profound concern was that the Lakota were losing their identity because of the concerted effort of the U.S. government and Christian missionaries to strip the Lakota of their culture. Lakota elders knew that once the core strength of an individual or a culture is weakened, there is vulnerability. And vulnerability does not always lead to positive consequences. In this case, for those old men, it did not seem that their children and grandchildren (and subsequent generations) would be able to retain their culture.

The transformation of the Lakota culture started in the 1840s, with the first generation of Lakota who had consistent contact with Euro-Americans. That contact began simply, unobtrusively, with a basic reason for human interaction: trade.

Convenience was the obvious benefit for the Lakota. Some of the goods they received from Euro-Americans, such as cloth and canvas, eliminated time and labor. The availability of cloth meant it was no longer necessary to hunt and skin deer and tan the hides for clothing. Likewise, canvas almost immediately replaced bison hides as material for lodge coverings, which meant women did not need to spend days processing green (raw) bison hides and more days sewing them together. One raw bison hide could weigh as much as two hundred pounds. A bolt of canvas was much lighter and could be used immediately.

Other items, such as skillets and kettles, made cooking easier. Flint and iron strikers (fire starters) could start fires more quickly than bow-drill fire starters. Steel needles were more durable than those made of bone or antler tips. Glass beads meant that women no longer needed to harvest, dry, and dye porcupine quills to decorate clothing and other items.

Strictly speaking, trading with whites meant that it was no longer necessary to perform labor-intensive, time-consuming tasks just to have a common tool, utensil, or article of clothing. Once enough Lakota people realized the benefit of interacting with Euro-Americans, the transformation of the Lakota culture was already under way.

Once the people felt it was acceptable to use the *things* of the whites, some were less resistant to the *ways* of the whites. The "maybe they are not that bad" way of thinking grew, creating a ready-made opportunity for Christian missionaries.

But the hearts, minds, and basic spiritual beliefs of the Lakota were not the only thing on the cusp of transformation. So were their lands. By the late 1840s and very early 1850s, white immigrants traveling west on the Oregon Trail from Missouri to Oregon, which cut through southern Lakota territory, were asking Congress for protection. Their fears were primarily a consequence of their own attitudes and actions toward native people, fueled by confrontations with the Lakota that they themselves had instigated or caused. That plea for help resulted in the 1851 Treaty of Fort Laramie gathering. The white "peace commissioners" representing the U.S. government arbitrarily drew boundary lines defining Lakota, Dakota, and Nakota territories; these new boundaries affected other tribes as well. The Americans, or Long Knives, as they were called by the Lakota, never backed down from their definition of Lakota territory.

Therefore, by the 1850s, the transformation of the Lakota was already well under way on several fronts. By the 1950s, at least three generations of Lakota had known nothing but life under the control of white authority and influence. Indeed, the conversation those old men were having about how the Lakota were changing occurred after an Episcopalian church service.

There was a wistfulness in conversations such as these, a yearning for things to be different in the lives of the conversationalists. There was always an underlying sadness in those moments, because the transformation these men were wrestling with was not of their choosing. I remember many such moments in my childhood. But I sensed that, in many ways, those old men (and old women) felt a deeper sadness for their children and grandchildren than they did for themselves. Those of us in subsequent generations would never know how it was in the old days. We would feel only the brunt of transformation brought by the change forced upon our culture. Because we had no place in the past, our sense of identity as Lakota people would be affected.

Many of the grandfathers I sat with that Sunday afternoon had—if not on that day, then on other occasions—expressed profound concern regarding the future of the Lakota as a people. They knew that change is a fact of life, an unavoidable reality, and unexpected or undesired transformation is, more often than not, its consequence. They were worried about the consequence of the change brought by Euro-Americans because of the immediate impact that change had had on their own grandparents' generation. They were afraid that their children and grandchildren, and subsequent generations, would be transformed into people barely resembling their ancestors. And some of their fears have come true.

In 1868, many Lakota leaders agreed to the terms of the treaty negotiated at Fort Laramie in what is now southeastern Wyoming. One of those conditions was that the Lakota were to live within the boundaries of the Great Sioux Reservation. This area was essentially the entire western half of what is now the state of South Dakota, bordered on the east by the Missouri River. They could continue to hunt in southeastern Montana, eastern Wyoming, and northern Nebraska. The Lakota were led to believe that this treaty was to last "as long as the waters flow and grasses grow."

However, in 1875, another "agreement" lopped off the western third of the Great Sioux Reservation—the part that included the Black Hills. A year before that, in 1874, the discovery of gold in the Black Hills was verified by a U.S. Army expedition led by Lieutenant Colonel George Custer. Two years later, in 1876, the Lakota and their allies would defeat him at the Battle of the Little Bighorn.

In 1877, only two Lakota bands roamed free, one under the leadership of Crazy Horse and the other under Sitting Bull. The latter group fled to Canada, hoping to avoid confrontation with the U.S. government and to find a new life. Crazy Horse capitulated in May of that year to avoid any further harm or hardship coming to his nine hundred or so followers, most of whom were women, children, and the elderly. They undertook the three-hundred-mile trek from what is now north-central Wyoming to Camp Robinson—the U.S.

Army outpost—in northwest Nebraska Territory. But if they expected conflict with the U.S. government to cease, they were disappointed.

There were already at least ten thousand Lakota people encamped at agencies on either side of Camp Robinson. Some of the headmen who had been appointed as "chiefs" by the army were jealous of Crazy Horse. They were afraid he could be appointed "chief" over all of them, and they would lose their status. To exacerbate the situation, the army suspected Crazy Horse would foment some kind of an uprising. They were afraid of him because his leadership at the Battle of Rosebud had stopped General George Cook in his tracks. Not to mention that Crazy Horse had been the principal military leader against the Seventh Cavalry at the Battle of Little Bighorn eight days later.

So when he and his people reached the camp in mid-May, Crazy Horse was met with jealousy on one hand and mistrust and fear on the other—a situation that escalated, fanned by rumor and innuendo. Some of the agency-appointed chiefs did everything they could to discredit him in the eyes of the Indian agents (white administrators of the U.S. Bureau of Indian Affairs) and army officers in charge.

In early September of 1877 the army issued orders for the arrest of Crazy Horse, and Lakota police were sent to apprehend him. After being escorted by an armed guard to Camp Robinson, Crazy Horse realized that he would be incarcerated. When he physically resisted, a melee broke out, and he was bayoneted by a soldier.

After Crazy Horse's murder, the U.S. government—more out of fear than logic—moved the various Lakota bands north into what was left of the Great Sioux Reservation. Indian Bureau officials were afraid of retaliation for Crazy Horse's death. Their intent was to scatter the various bands across the landscape in order to minimize any contact they would have with one another.

In 1889, the U.S. Congress passed the Sioux Act, which created six distinct reservations. The Hunkpapa occupied the Standing Rock Reservation in the north-central portion of what would become the state of South Dakota. Adjacent and to the south were the Mniconju, Itazipacola, Sihasapa, and Oohenunpa bands on the Cheyenne River Reservation. The Sicangu were given the Rosebud Sioux Reservation, in the south-central portion of the later-to-be state, and the Oglala moved into the southwest area, onto the Pine Ridge Reservation. A splinter group from the Sicangu (Rosebud) became the inhabitants of the Lower Brule Reservation, by far the smallest reservation, along the Missouri.

Less than fifty years after the Fort Laramie Treaty of 1868, the Great Sioux Reservation was no more. Lands not regarded as reservations were removed from Lakota ownership, meaning that eleven million acres of land from the original single reservation were lost.

Territorial change was constant and traumatic for the Lakota, but so, too, were changes in Lakota societal structure. Children were put in school by the U.S. government, either on the reservation or off. Off-reservation schools included Carlisle Indian Industrial School in Carlisle, Pennsylvania, over a thousand miles away from the northern plains. Its headmaster, Henry Pratt, was a former army captain whose policy was to "kill the Indian and save the man." Two, perhaps three, of the old men talking on that Sunday afternoon had been sent to Carlisle as boys and had returned home angry young men.

Missionaries of every denomination ran amuck, anxious to "save" Lakota souls. Lakota medicine men, the traditional healers and spiritual leaders, were not permitted to do their work. The Catholics built boarding schools on every reservation, and they and government boarding schools banned the speaking of the Lakota language. The government outlawed all traditional ceremonies, including the Sun Dance, the most sacred ceremony of the Lakota.

In 1887, before the Sioux Act, the U.S. Congress passed the Dawes Severalty Act, also called the Homestead Act, which individualized ownership of Indian land within the reservations. A census was conducted, and reservation lands were surveyed. Married Lakota men were allotted 160 acres, and single men eighteen years of age and older were allotted 80 acres. Land left over—the surplus—was opened to white homesteading. By 1910, the Dawes Act had brought a new reality to every reservation in South Dakota: white ownership of land *within* reservation borders. From that moment, white land ownership within reservations steadily increased. By the 1970s, Lakota on the Rosebud Reservation owned 40 percent and whites owned 60 percent in four of the five counties. Increased white land ownership led to the diminishment of the 1881 reservation boundary. Today, the Rosebud Sioux Indian Reservation is one-fifth its original area, its boundaries coinciding with one of the sixty-seven counties in the state.

In 1889 and 1890, there was one overt and tragic reaction to forced change: the coming of the Ghost Dance. It is commonly referred to as an "uprising," and although that label may be semantically correct, the Ghost Dance did not start as such. From the beginning, the U.S. government woefully misunderstood the Ghost Dance phenomenon, mistakenly assuming it was martial in nature. Whatever else it was or was thought to be, at heart it was a protest.

By 1890, the circumstances for all native people in the West could be summed up in one word: *overwhelmed*. They had been overwhelmed by a nation with more technology than they had and with a sense of racial superiority that fostered an attitude of entitlement. Mostly, however, it was an issue of numbers. All of the tribes and nations of native people in the West numbered less than a million, and the population of the United States of America was over twenty-five million. Even if the native people had been adequately armed and equipped for all-out war, the numerical odds were too high. Therefore, by 1890, most native nations in the West had lost much or all of their lands, their cultures had been weakened or destroyed, and their ways of life were gone. It is no wonder then that a tiny spark of hope quickly became a flame.

The spark was a vision experienced by a part-Paiute holy man during an eclipse of the sun in northern Nevada in 1888.

Wovoka was his Paiute name, Jack Wilson his white name, and his vision was simple. In it, he saw a world that had returned to what it was before the coming of the white people, when all native people lived free and game was abundant. He told everyone that it was possible to bring back that world by dancing and praying to their ancestors—performing a Ghost Dance. If the dancers were sufficiently sincere, the ancestors would listen and restore the world to what it had been.

The Ghost Dance caught on, spreading from the southwest, and found ardent followers on the north-central plains, notably among the Lakota. It spread not because native people saw it as a way to militarily overthrow the whites, but because the participants were tired of the status quo, tired of white authority. Dancing—instead of fighting—seemed to be *the* way to bring back the old ways. Those who danced believed that it would bring about Wovoka's vision. Furthermore, it was an opportunity for individual men and women to act on their feelings of frustration, anger, fear, and mistrust. It was, no more and no less, an act of protest, a protest against not only the changes—loss of land, lifestyle, and the bison; white control; railroads; missionaries; schools—but also (or perhaps mainly) against the transformation in the people that those changes were causing. The scariest change was the advent of a new identity that many farsighted Lakota saw as neither Lakota nor white.

The Ghost Dance ended tragically. U.S. government officials turned it into a military uprising because they grossly misjudged and overreacted to the dancing and what it signified. They certainly misjudged Sitting Bull's role in it. He was murdered because of their mistake.

On the morning of December 15, 1890, about forty Indian policemen arrived at Sitting Bull's log house on the Standing Rock Reservation to arrest him. The U.S. government wanted to incarcerate him in order to prevent him from influencing his fellow Hunkpapa Lakota to participate in the Ghost Dance. The U.S. government believed that any Ghost Dancer—man, woman, or child—was a threat.

Emotions were high at Sitting Bull's camp, not because of the Ghost Dance, but because the Indian police were arresting him. He was at first cooperative; then he berated the commander of the police contingent, a Hunkpapa Lakota. Sitting Bull's family and supporters gathered quickly, and the police attempted to escort him through the crowd. Insults, shouts, and a scuffle broke out, and then shots were fired. Indian policemen fell, some mortally wounded. Tragically, Sitting Bull was shot as well by one of the dying policemen.

Two weeks later, the U.S. Army killed nearly three hundred Lakota, mostly women and children, at Wounded Knee Creek— Lakota who were simply trying to find shelter from the storm of change. All of these tragic events were part of the transformation of a culture.

Eighty years later, only 30 percent of the Lakota population spoke their native language, and many were third- or fourth-generation Christians. Lakota children were learning Lakota history from white teachers in white-controlled school systems.

And they were known to the world at large by a name not from their language: the Sioux.

Those old Lakota men sitting in the shade of a cottonwood tree on that Sunday afternoon did not like the changes—changes not of their choosing—that their people had endured for a hundred years. They were profoundly worried, even fearful, that those changes would transform future generations into unrecognizable and perhaps even lesser versions of their ancestors. Those old men spoke entirely in Lakota that day. Nearly sixty years later, when I have similar conversations with Lakota relatives and friends, and we express the same fears and worries, we speak in English.

Change has transformed us as a culture. It was in the process of doing so when those old men expressed their concerns and fears. The fact that they had sat for an hour in an Episcopalian church service listening to prayers and a sermon in English was at least one indication of that transformation. That they were dressed in wool and calico was another, and that there were Chevrolets, Fords, and Dodges parked under the trees, instead of horses, was one more.

The fears of those old men have come to pass. We Lakota have been transformed. But *what* we have been transformed into is a question yet to be answered.

Furthermore, the history of the Lakota transformation and its consequences is a cautionary tale for everyone, because change and transformation are part of our lives, individually and collectively.

THE SKILL OF THE BOW MAKER, THE RESILIENCE OF THE TREE

That tale of Lakota transformation in the face of changing circumstances is, for me, represented by the crafting of a simple ash-wood bow and a willow arrow.

Every tool, utensil, article of clothing, every object and product that we use or that is a part of our everyday existence is the end result of several kinds of raw materials. Those raw materials must be gathered, mined, procured, harvested, or otherwise obtained. After that comes the preparation and manufacture of the object. Most of us are not aware of that process. I am reminded of the man who, when asked where milk and meat came from, replied, "The grocery store." Or another who thought that window glass was dug out of a mine.

In the spring of 1950, when I saw my grandfather's ash bow and willow arrows for the first time, I was enthralled by them but had no idea how they came to be. I was five at the time, but by the age of seven, I knew exactly what bows and arrows were made from and how they were made. As a young adult, I realized that the transformation of ash (or oak or chokecherry) into a bow and willow stalks into arrows represented many circumstances and events in our lives.

A tree or sometimes a branch is *transformed* into a bow. But such a simple statement, no matter the depth of its reality, does not begin to reveal the process an ash, oak, or chokecherry tree is subjected to in order to become a bow.

There are several steps in the process.

Lakota bow makers (bowyers) wanted a tree as straight and as free of knots and branches as possible, and a tree at least as tall as a grown man. Over the summer and autumn, the bowyers searched through groves of ash and oak and thickets of chokecherry shrubs along creeks and rivers. Most Lakota bow makers preferred chokecherry because it was a fine-grained hardwood and more flexible than ash or oak. But it was extremely difficult to find a chokecherry tree tall enough or straight enough to make into a bow. The next preference was lone oaks—individual trees growing apart from oak thickets, which meant they were always taller than other oaks. Comparatively, however, oaks tended to be thicker than ash trees of the same age. Since ash trees were more abundant on the northern plains and easier to work than oak, ash was used more often.

Once a likely tree was selected, the bow maker marked it and then returned to cut the tree during or after the midwinter moon (December), when the sap was down. The bottom of the cut tree, the end closest to the roots, was marked with a deep groove.

Bow makers did not necessarily cut bow wood every winter. They usually did so only when their supply of staves (the harvested trees split lengthwise) was finished curing.

It was the winter after my grandfather built our log house on the plateau above the Little White River when we cut down an ash tree. I was five years old, and in late January or early February, I accompanied him down into a gully west of our house. It was a cold night sometime after the new moon because I remember my breath was misting small clouds in front of me.

The quarter moon was well above the horizon, as I recall. But the inside of the gully was shadowy, and the snow made the hillside slick and treacherous. My job was to carry the kerosene lantern, so we could pick our way through without falling. We found the small ash tree my grandfather had marked in the autumn. With a few expert strokes of the axe, my grandfather cut down the tree. From his pocket, he took out a small bundle of tobacco and told me to leave it on the stump. It was an offering for the life of the tree. He told me to say thank you to the tree, and I did.

After he trimmed off the branches, he cut the tree to length, about as tall as he was. Back at the house, we left the small log propped beside the front porch. I imagine, with the exceptions of the steel axe, the kerosene lantern, and our log house, our little foray into the gully to cut that tree was no different from those of many previous generations of Lakota grandfathers and grandsons who cut bow trees on a cold winter night.

The next step, then and now, was to split the log. Depending on its diameter, it could yield up to four staves. In the past, the staves were hung below the smoke hole of the bow maker's bison-hide lodge to begin the curing process. Lakota bison-hide lodges were conical in shape, so warm air rose to the top. Hanging the staves where they would receive the benefits of the escaping smoke and warm air was the preferred method of curing, and staves were allowed to dry in this manner for at least three years. In the 1950s, my grandparents and I did not live in a bison-hide lodge, so my grandfather hung one of the two staves from his log horizontally against the wall on two large nails behind the big iron cook-stove. Sadly, that particular stave never became a bow because we moved away from that log house before it was finished curing. The other stave he kept outside in the cold, so it would stay green.

After three years of air-drying, staves were ready to be shaped into bows. This task was simple, but labor intensive. After removing the bark, the bow maker drew on the stave an outline of the shape of the bow (using cooled charcoal embers from the fire) and then began to shave away the excess wood.

Sometime before my sixth birthday, in the Moon When the Geese Return (early April), my grandfather started working on the green stave, the one he had kept outside under the snow. I recall asking him what he was doing. He said there was a bow in the stave, and it was his job to find it, to bring it out. To do that, he had to remove all the wood in the way.

In pre-reservation days, making bows was either a winter-night activity or a summertime task. Hours of daylight were shorter in the winter, so bow makers worked in their lodges by the light of the inside fire. Those who preferred the summer would work by a flowing stream, in which they would soak the stave occasionally to soften up the outer layer of the wood and make carving or shaving easier. I think the latter was the most popular method for carving in the days of stone tools.

My grandfather's tools were a large knife, which he sharpened frequently as he worked, and a wood rasp. He worked on the stave in the afternoons and evenings, often sitting beneath the willow-shade arbor on the north side of our house, after our chores were done, and he worked slowly. My boyhood impatience notwithstanding, it took about a week for him to finish the bow—my bow. My job was to gather up the wood shavings and put them into a burlap bag.

To my six-year-old eyes, that bow was the most beautiful thing I had ever seen. It was probably about forty inches long. I never measured it because at the time my grandfather made it, I had not started school yet and so knew nothing about rulers or inches. As a matter of fact, no kind of ruler was part of my grandfather's bow-making tools. His bow, the one he had made months before, was longer and wider. Lakota bows were made according to the size of their shooters. Logically, then, a short archer's bow was not as long as one for a tall man.

Even after my grandfather had finished carving the stave into a bow, it was not yet finished, I was surprised to learn. My grandfather explained that he was using something of a shortcut, a faster way of making a bow that avoided the years of curing staves usually required.

The day after he finished carving, we built a large fire outside, starting it with the wood shavings I had collected. We kept that fire going from morning to well after sundown. My new bow was propped on a makeshift platform above it. My job was to turn it from front to back and then back to front when my grandfather told me to, about every hour or so.

I noticed that the bow was turning from a creamy white to yellow the longer it hung above the fire. When I asked why we were cooking my bow, my grandfather said it was to make it harder and strong.

That night, we brought the bow inside, and the next morning, he inspected it closely and bent it over his knee. After removing more material, we built the fire again and hung the bow over it for two more days. Then my grandfather declared the bow to be finished. He added a sinew string, and I had my first bow.

Sometime during the process of making the bow, we had trekked down to the Little White River, about two miles from our house, and cut about a dozen river-willow stalks. Each was about thirty inches in length and as thick as my grandfather's little finger. Crafting one of those stalks into an arrow did not take nearly as long as making a bow, but doing all twelve took several days.

The first step was to strip off the bark. Then my grandfather pulled the bare stalks through what is known as a sizer. In this case, the sizer was a slab of hardwood with a hole in it, probably slightly larger than a quarter-inch in diameter. Pulling the green shaft through the hole compressed the entire length of the stalk—from the top down to the bottom, the end closest to the root—to the same width. The result was a shaft of uniform width along its entire length, except for one end. The bottom or root end became the string notch, or nock.

After that, my grandfather hand-straightened the stalks and hung them behind the cookstove. A couple days later, he hand-straightened them again, this time after holding them over the outside fire. Straightening occurred more than once with several of the stalks, until all the shafts were as straight as the rays of the sun.

Then my grandfather cut them all to length, some long enough for him and some short enough for me. The method of measurement for our respective arrows was the same: the arrow was as long as the distance from the corner of the bent elbow to the tip of the middle finger, plus the width of a hand.

After cutting a narrow notch into the tip (the arrowhead end), he attached feathers beneath the nock. He had split black crow feathers down the middle with a knife and cut each to a length of about four inches. After trimming the quills, he attached one feather at a time, using hide glue and thin strands of sinew.

My grandfather then attached bone points, carved from deer ribs, to four of my arrows. Each point was about two-inches long and probably half an inch at its widest point, just before the shank. The shank was fitted into the notch he'd carved at the tip, held in place with hide glue, and then wrapped with strands of sinew. It took two days for the glue to dry and set. (The next year, he made hunting arrows for me, and those were tipped with iron heads.)

As time went by and I reminisced with the mind, heart, and experiences of an adult, I realized that within my fond recollections of my grandfather's bow and arrow making, there was a lesson, both for me and for anyone who has experienced change.

Life is a series of transformations. Some occur slowly, like the transformation the stave undergoes as it is cured for years before being crafted into a bow. Others occur quickly, like the one the green stave went through as my grandfather carved it, then cured and hardened it with fire.

Transformations, small or significant, are part of our lives. Sometimes we remember them because of the hardship and pain that caused them or with which we experienced them. Other times transformations occur that we might not even be aware of.

Now, at the age of sixty-five, I frequently think about what the ash tree and river willows were forced to sacrifice in order to be crafted—transformed—into a bow and arrows. They gave up their very lives, their vibrancy. Yet their essence—the basic, real, and invariable nature of these trees—lived on in the bows.

What was it about the ash tree (or the oak and the chokecherry) that made a good bow? What made an ash, oak, or chokecherry bow the kind of weapon with which a man could confidently chase game and face his enemies? Some of the finished bow's quality had to with the bow maker's skill, but most of it came from the wood, the essence of the tree. Flexibility is what makes hardwoods good bow material. But there is another quality that enables the bow to function in all kinds of weather, under all manner of harsh conditions: resiliency.

Fortunately, resiliency is not limited to ash trees. It is a quality anything or anyone, including cultures and individuals, can learn or develop.

Just as trees are transformed by bow makers, we Lakota, and every other native tribe and nation on this continent, are still being transformed as a consequence of interaction with Europeans and Euro-Americans. Like the trees, we have sacrificed the vibrancy, the lives of our cultures, that which made us uniquely who and what we were for generations untold. Like the tree whose growth and flowering stopped the moment the bow maker's axe bit into its flesh, our growth and flowering stopped the moment our territories and resources were coveted by Europeans and Euro-Americans.

But there are differences between trees and us, and between bow makers and the Europeans and Euro-Americans as well. Though the Lakota bow makers took the lives of trees, they did not do that with any sense of superiority, entitlement, or animosity. Thereafter, they approached their task respectfully and somberly, making sure that factors in their lives were good and in balance before they began, because they believed that they imbued the bow with what they were feeling. For example, if there was stress or tragedy in their lives, they refrained from making bows. When they were ready, they prayed before they began their task. Next, they applied their knowledge and skills to make the best possible bow they could.

Europeans and Euro-Americans have not brought change upon the native peoples with the same self-reflection, respect, and care. Instead, they are like a bow maker who takes shortcuts because of impatience, or who does not stick to tried-and-true designs, or who simply does not have the skill to create a good bow. The result is a bow that is not balanced; one limb is more stressed than the other when the bow is drawn, and, sooner rather than later, it breaks.

The ultimate outcome of the transformation of native tribes and nations in North America (and South America, for that matter) remains to be seen, because there are other realities that should not be overlooked. There are instances when transformation is intentional, undertaken to change something completely, to render it entirely different from the original. Those who cause such transformation have self-serving reasons for doing so. Europeans and Euro-Americans wanting to "civilize" North and South American natives tried—and are still trying—to transform us into versions of themselves, so they can feel more comfortable.

Because the end result of transformation is not always positive for everyone involved, some (hopefully, many) feel that the outcome of the transformation of the native peoples resulting from the interaction with Europeans and Euro-Americans remains to be seen. In my opinion, those of us who think this way are the resilient ones.

Tragically, there are native peoples who have capitulated to outside forces by forsaking their own cultures and becoming that which has forced (and is forcing) the transformation. They are like the shavings that fall when the bow maker carves the bow. They are simply by-products of the process, no longer connected to the essence of the tree.

Those of us who struggle to be resilient ensure that, in spite of the transformation forced upon us for several generations, the essence, the best of our culture, will be retained. Our resilience ensures that our cultures will endure even though, like the tree, we did not choose to be transformed, and even though our transformation was brought on by ignorant, impatient, and unskilled hands.

In the end, resilience can be more the consequence of the tree than the skill of the bow maker.

To Choose to Change

Rumor has it that preliminary reports from the 2010 U.S. Census indicate that the Native American population in this country is at just over four million, double what it was in 2000. But that figure is regarded skeptically in the native community for one simple reason: the U.S. Census does not ask for verification of race. There was no way that a census worker could technically or legally question or verify a blue-eyed or light-skinned person's assertion that he or she is native. There was also no way to verify claims made in writing.

Numbers aside, who is a Native American these days, given the effect of generations of assimilation and acculturation? To be Indian, Native American, or American Indian is to be an enrolled member of a federally recognized tribe or nation, and someone needs to have a minimum amount of native blood in order to be enrolled. For most tribes, that amount is one-fourth, and for others, it is one-eighth. In other words, it is possible for a person to be enrolled in federally recognized Tribe X if that individual can verify that he or she has at least one-fourth (25 percent) tribal blood, through one parent or both. That means the enrollee is biologically three-fourths something else—a racial mixture of other native tribes and/or non-native blood—but still legally a member of Tribe X. However, being legally enrolled in a native tribe is not the same as being culturally or traditionally native, as was glaringly evident on the part of several men who worked for the U.S. government, supposedly as Indian or native advocates.

The U.S. Bureau of Indian Affairs (BIA) was established in 1824 and housed in the Department of War (now Department of Defense). In 1849, it was moved to the Department of the Interior. The BIA is run by a commissioner, an undersecretary of the Department of the Interior.

The commissioner of the BIA serves at the pleasure of the president of the United States and is, therefore, an appointee. The first appointees were all white men. In 1868, however, a native person was appointed BIA commissioner. He was Ely Parker, a member of the Seneca Nation, whose home territory is now upstate New York.

Parker was appointed to the post by President Ulysses S. Grant as a result of his service in the Civil War. Parker was an aide to then General Grant, rose to the rank of brigadier general in the Union Army, and was present at Lee's surrender at Appomattox Court House. In fact, Parker transcribed the surrender papers. Parker's service as commissioner of the BIA was not a highlight of his career, due to political sniping by his and President Grant's opponents.

In the twentieth century, well after the federal government had established blood-degree criteria for enrollment in federally recognized tribes, there were BIA commissioner appointees who were legally Indian or native. All were men, and all barely met the minimum blood-degree requirement; some were from tribes with the one-eighth minimum requirement. They may have been one-eighth Indian in the eyes of the law, but their other seven-eighths were culturally white. Most (if not all) of those appointees had no cultural ties to their tribe of enrollment—meaning they did not have the experiences of those who grew up in traditional or reservation communities. Such individuals were "safe" for the administration in power to appoint because they belonged to the requisite political party and were more non-native than they were native. They definitely did not rock the boat. It is questionable where the loyalties of Commissioner One-eighth Indian and Seven-eighths White, a dues-paying member of the Republican or Democratic Party, lay. Was he more loyal to his political party and the president who appointed him or to the loose or nonexistent ties he might have felt to the tribe of his enrollment?

There were a few native appointees who did have strong cultural ties with their ancestral tribes, but they were few and far between.

There are currently over 480 ethnically identifiable indigenous tribes or nations in the United States. Most of them have federal recognition—that is, the U.S. government recognizes that they exist. Of those that are not federally recognized, most never had federal recognition, while some did but lost it for one reason or another.

Among the ethnically identifiable tribes, approximately 160 native languages are spoken, which means that about 320 tribes no longer have a living language.

Thirty-one of the fifty states have Indian reservations, mostly federal and a few state reservations.

All of the foregoing facts are consequences of transformation.

Moreover, this transformation is still ongoing. It is anyone's guess as to why it is not complete, but native people might tell you that the transformation process itself is the reason.

In the late 1800s, the U.S. government launched an intensive policy of assimilation. The word *assimilate* means "to take in and incorporate as one's own, absorb; to bring into conformity with the customs and attitudes of a dominant cultural group."

Nothing in that definition or in the implementation of the government's policy of assimilation offered meaningful choices to those being assimilated. Native people were going to become hardworking and productive members of American society, as well as reasonable facsimiles of white Americans, and that was that. Hence, the outlawing of native customs, traditions, and religious practices; the forcible removal of native people from their homelands; and the placement of native children in government and parochial schools, not to mention the bans on native languages in those boarding schools.

Generally speaking, native people were made to feel shame about their race, and many were individually persecuted. For example, early missionaries criticized and ridiculed native spiritual beliefs and caused doubt and uncertainty in children and young people. At the schools they were sent to, those same children and young people were punished if they were caught speaking their native language. The message was loud and clear: being native was unacceptable.

There are also those who had little choice but to assimilate. There were and are native children placed in or adopted by white families. Those children were and are inculcated with the values and traditions of the adoptive families. In many cases, the adoptive parents make no attempt to connect the children with their racial and cultural heritage or any of their extended biological families.

In 1924, the U.S. Congress granted American citizenship to native people, citing it as a reward for natives serving in the armed forces during World War I. Congress did not bother to ask if native people wanted to be American citizens, and the move was perceived by many native people as another attempt to erode their identity. Then, in 1934, Congress passed the Indian Reorganization Act (IRA), which, among other things, created a form of self-government for native tribes, patterned after the United States. Never mind that native tribes were successfully governing themselves hundreds of years before the Declaration of Independence was a gleam in Thomas Jefferson's eye. Over the course of just a few generations, the IRA effectively obliterated the experience- and wisdom-based government and leadership systems that had long existed in many native tribes.

The intensity of the assimilative process aimed at native people began to wane in the 1960s, though many white teachers, counselors, and others still maintained—and still hold—the attitude that native students could "better" themselves by being like everyone else. Even the 1960s television show *Gunsmoke* got into the act. Marshal Matt Dillon gave his sage counsel to two young men who were part Indian, telling them it was possible to be good people in spite of being part Indian.

But in the process of carrying out the policy of assimilation, the U.S. government learned a basic fact about human nature: the harder you try to take something away from people, the harder they hang on. That is basically why there are still native tribes and nations whose people are culturally, experientially, and in every other way connected to who and what they had been before the Europeans arrived.

Native Americans, American Indians, or just plain Indians today are part of the American mainstream. In many ways, we are like everyone else who wears the label of *American*. We are parents, grandparents, widows, widowers, sons, daughters, grandchildren, students. We are teachers, construction workers, physicians, athletes, performers, lawyers, electricians, retailers, artists, politicians, writers, pastors, plumbers, traditional healers, sports fans, readers, truck drivers, moviegoers, and so on and so on. We no longer live in bison-hide dwellings, longhouses, or cliff dwellings. Nor do we chase whales on the ocean in long boats or bison on the plains on horseback. What is left of our lands is marked by lines on a map and not by natural landmarks. We live in apartments, condominiums, modular homes, or frame houses, and we do pursue careers and have jobs (if we are lucky) or generally just try to get by—like everyone else.

But there is another dimension to us: the connection to our tribal heritage, customs, and traditions. Though we are not the only group of people to have a connection to our history and ancestry, that connection is, for us, an especially significant part of our identity today, one that is a source of pride. Though we have been transformed to an extent, we have found ways to be native while we contribute to American society and fulfill that society's roles and expectations. That is nothing more or less than what we have been doing for ages.

Some of us—no matter our indigenous tribe or nation—have accepted the reality that time and circumstances have transformed us. The old, pre-European lifestyles will not come back (at least not in the foreseeable future), but the core of who and what we were as Lakota—or as Diné, Tsalagi, Inuit, Miccosoukee, and so on—remains. Once we realize that, we can accept the most profound reality we have—that we can and should make the most of the aspects of our cultures that have survived. And what has survived is enough for us to continue being who and what we are. After all, the archer who shoots the bow knows that it is made from an ash, or oak, or chokecherry tree, and each tree has its own positive characteristics. By the same token, the archer knows the arrow is made from willow or young chokecherry. Neither the bow nor the arrow stops being ash or oak or chokecherry or willow simply because it has been transformed.

Part of the reason our culture survives, despite the assimilation efforts, is that we took as much control as possible over the process of transformation. A basic aspect of human nature is that when we freely make a choice or feel that something is our idea, we take ownership of our decision and, consequently, work harder to bring it to fruition. That is the reason Native Americans (or American Indians) are part of the mainstream of America. Most of us realize that we can pick and choose and have control over our individual lives as citizens and human beings. Because of the relationship our tribal governments have with the states and the federal government, we may still be stuck with circa nineteenth-century ethnocentric and paternalistic attitudes; however, we are here in the twenty-first century as individuals who, for the most part, choose to be who we are, building on the foundation of what we are.

Therein lies a lesson for each of us, native or non-native: We can be aware of the transformation process happening to us and exercise as much control over it as we can. In that sense, we would be like the bow maker who approaches his task thoughtfully, respectfully, and skillfully in order to produce the best possible bow. But in order to positively affect our lives, we must have the insight to know the difference between aspects of transformation that are good for us and aspects that are not. When we approach our transformation with that insight, we are using *acculturation* rather than allowing *assimilation*.

Acculturation is the process of adopting, by choice, the cultural traits or social patterns of another group. The reason some Native Americans still have a strong connection to who and what we *have been* is that we chose the path of acculturation— we chose to affect what we were becoming—no matter what the proponents of assimilation were trying to do. Making this choice is a large reason we have arrived in the twenty-first century with most of our sense of cultural identity intact. Neither acculturation nor assimilation is easy or harmless, but choosing to transform is far more beneficial than being forced to, because it allows us to select the qualities of another group that appeal to and are useful to us.

That generation of native people who were the first to confront reservation life, beginning in the late 1860s west of the Mississippi River, faced a harsh initial shock. Cultural traditions, norms, customs, beliefs, and language, they were told, had to be forgotten. They were literally a captive audience, and they had to react to the sudden change in lifestyle and cope with the everyday necessity of survival. They had little time or opportunity to analyze the process forced upon them. Instead of tanned hides, they wore cotton and wool. Instead of moccasins, they wore stiff leather shoes. Instead of performing familiar and ingrained religious ceremonies, they were forced to worship in new ways every seventh day. Their children, the next generation, were affected by the ways in which their parents endured, adapted to, or accepted forced change.

Those who endured and clung to their Lakota ways and identity did so because they found a way to adapt. They outwardly lived the way the U.S. government and the missionaries wanted them to, but inwardly, they hung on to the language, beliefs, customs, and traditions that made them Lakota. They turned assimilation into acculturation and taught their children to do the same.

Those who accepted most or all aspects of the new ways, for all intents and purposes, gave up their culture and influenced their children to do the same.

The fact that there is still a viable Lakota culture is a consequence of acculturation. This is the reason that our Lakota Sun Dance is performed just as often today, if not more often, than it was in the pre-reservation era. Today's participants may ride to a Sun Dance in sedans and SUVs rather than on horses, pitch nylon tents alongside canvas tipis, and sit in lawn chairs rather than willow chairs, but their hearts and minds are the same as those of their ancestors.

FACES IN THE WATER OF CHANGE

As native people today, are we a better or stronger version of what we once were? Or are we just different because of history and circumstance?

Understandably, the answer will vary depending on which native person you ask.

The parallel question for everyone is, can people become better and stronger? Can individuals, societies, cultures, and nations become better and stronger?

Perhaps the following story will help us find the answers. Iktomi, more commonly known as the Trickster, is the subject of many stories designed to offer a lesson or moral. One of those stories fits the theme of this particular discussion.

Iktomi was not a hunter or a fisherman or a planter of crops or a builder of dwellings. His lot in life was to live on his wits. Consequently, he was always needy in some way.

On one beautiful afternoon, after he awoke in a deserted den in a hillside, he decided to take a walk. He was thinking that he might find some food somewhere. Iktomi walked down the hill, and there he came upon a pond with clear blue water, which was fortunate because he happened to be thirsty. As he lay on his belly to sip the water, Iktomi saw a reflection on the pond's surface. After a moment of confusion, he realized it was his own face he saw.

Iktomi was pleased to see himself in the water, especially since he thought himself handsome. He spent the rest of the day admiring his reflection. After the sun went down, he went back to the den in the hillside.

He went back to the pond the next afternoon. Though the sun was shining, it was windy, and the surface of the water had small waves. Ignoring the wind, Iktomi lay down and looked into the water. Instead of the handsome face he expected to see, he saw a distorted one. In a bit of disbelief, he closed his eyes and opened them again, only to see a face in the water bending and stretching. After pondering the situation for several long moments, Iktomi decided the strange reflection in the water was not his.

Disgusted, he decided to look for food to get a new perspective. He feasted on berries in a chokecherry thicket and then took a nap. The wind had carried in rain clouds, and drops began falling, some on Iktomi's face. Soon there was a steady rain. Iktomi felt a chill and awoke from his nap. Irritated at the rain, he hurried away toward his den.

As luck would have it, he passed by the pond. The rain was falling hard; the water in the pond was gray, and all the raindrops made it murky. Still, Iktomi knelt at the water's edge to see if his reflection was there. A dark, indistinguishable shadow peeked back at him. The shadow had no eyes, no nose, and no mouth. It was only a dark blob. A little frightened, Iktomi jumped away and hurried back to his den to get out of the rain, all the while wondering whose reflection he had seen. It certainly was not his.

Iktomi awoke the next afternoon. He was hungry again, but also angry. He was certain that the pond was playing tricks on him. As he paced inside a thicket, Rabbit happened by and cautiously greeted the Trickster. It was a fortunate meeting, since Iktomi wanted to talk to someone about the pond. He summed up his not-so-satisfactory encounters with the pond, complaining that it was showing him reflections that were not real.

Rabbit pondered Iktomi's story for a moment and came to a conclusion. He revealed to Iktomi that all of the reflections were indeed his, but each appeared different, and even strange, because of the sun, the wind, and the rain.

This answer, of course, did nothing to enlighten Iktomi. Which of those reflections was he to believe, if they were all of him, he asked Rabbit.

Rabbit's response was simple and truthful. There was no choice but to believe them all, no matter how good or bad or strange they appeared to be.

And then Rabbit offered one final bit of advice: "If you do not know who you are, then it does not matter what you believe."

There are a variety of ways to define what *better* and *stronger* may mean for native people or people in general. Can anything or anyone that is basically good build on that positive characteristic, that goodness, and improve? Something or someone that is negative can, within the broad context of improvement, become more negative. Therefore, in a world society where positivity and goodness are preferable, we are talking about two different kinds of transformation: we want good to become even better, and we want the negative to change to something good.

Is the first kind of transformation possible? If the foundation for the anyone or anything in question is positive or good, can that anyone or anything become better?

To begin to formulate an answer, we need to return to the opening question of this section: as native people today, are we a better or stronger version of what we once were?

The first part of the answer is that clearly we are different in many ways.

Our land base is much smaller—laughably smaller—and is relegated to nearly 250 reservations. According to BIA statistics, 60 percent of Native Americans live off reservations and 40 percent live on reservations. Inside the boundaries of that land base, we adhere to the laws, rules, regulations, and practices of the culture that diminished our lands. That means very, very few of us modern North American natives live the same lifestyle our ancestors did. Where our ancestors lived and how they lived off and with the land determined their lifestyles. Where and how we live today is determined by the same job and career choices everyone else in North American society faces.

Our racial composition is much more varied than it was in pre-European days. Not only have we mixed with Europeans and other non-North American peoples, but we have also mixed more with other native tribes. It is not unusual, then, for a contemporary native person to have not only a biracial background, but a multitribal one as well. For example, a person's ancestral background might be a mix of Lakota (Sioux), Diné (Navajo), and Sahiyela (Cheyenne), as well as French and Scottish.

Our villages in the past were nomadic or sedentary. The village—regardless of whether its dwellings were made of hide, snow and ice, stone, thatch, or wood—was the first, most consistent, and strongest influence on everyone in it. No matter what tribe they were part of, our ancestors effectively practiced the concept that "it takes a village to raise a child." Few of us are part of the dynamic of the village, the community consisting of the extended families, anymore. Since the 1960s, Western reservations have had "housing projects" through the U.S. Department of Housing and Urban Development (HUD). Houses were built in locations selected by HUD and the tribal housing program. Living in a given location was not determined by familial or community relationships, biological or otherwise. Applicants for housing were and are selected on the basis of need and income level. Economics and regulations, as well as tribal politics, are the prime considerations these days.

However, a new dynamic has stepped in: instant communication. Technology has enabled scattered native families to keep in touch, whether we live on or off the reservation. E-mail, cell phones, and texting are likely the new ties that bind, but they will never replace Grandma and Grandpa's embrace.

While the positive program of providing affordable housing has created, in many cases, a negative consequence for the traditional village, a different kind of effort changed another aspect of native cultures. Native religion and spirituality were in the crosshairs of targeted change (as mentioned earlier). Today, native people have a variety of religious beliefs other than traditional ancestral beliefs. Some of us are Baha'i, some of us are Buddhists, and some of us have joined other sects and acquired other beliefs as well. Christianity, in different denominations, maintains a strong presence on many reservations. Since the 1950s, native people have risen from the church rank and file to become pastors and priests.

Two particular aspects of native life have been transformed significantly: law and education. Both Indian law and Indian education had much different connotations in the pre-European, pre-reservation era. Law was ingrained in the codes of social conduct that had evolved over generations, and native societies had ways and means of dealing with offensive conduct and crime. It is interesting to note that crimes such as assault and murder were not major or consistent problems for many native tribes. Judgment and punishment for such crimes were not extremely harsh, but they were inflexible. Once judgment was passed and a sentence imposed—essentially by the entire village or community—there was no changing it or turning back, and this inflexibility probably contributed to the scarcity of violent crime.

Indian law today is based on acts of Congress, which have created a set of conditions and circumstances within which native tribes and nations are compelled to function. On another level, but no less important, are the laws enacted by or for tribes since the Indian Reorganization Act of 1934. These are the basis for the tribal codes by which tribal courts function.

Indian education, like law, was different before Europeans came. Native societies employed effective approaches for teaching children and young people to be self-sufficient, caring, and productive members of society. By and large, education was usually a one-on-one process of instruction and mentoring: girls and young women were taught by their mothers, grandmothers, and aunts; boys were taught by their fathers, uncles, and grandfathers. In addition to providing children with a basic education, such a system fostered self-confidence and a sense of place in the village, community, and society.

Indian education as we know it today began in the infamous boarding school era, when native children were forcibly placed in schools established or authorized by the U.S. government, and educating native children was the way to indoctrinate them in Euro-American culture. It was also the way to strip away their culture from them. For those reasons and more— including the fact that it meant children spent months or years away from home and family, received harsh treatment and punishments, and were subjected to emotional, verbal, and sexual abuse—Euro-American education did not win the hearts and minds of native people. By and large, native children and their families endured this enforced educational system because they were powerless to change it.

Change arguably began in the 1960s, as native families and communities began to speak up against the rigidity of educational policies and misguided curricula and against the insensitivity of school administrators and teachers. By then, natives were graduating from colleges and universities and beginning to return to native communities with much more awareness of the educational process. Some were teachers. In the late 1960s, a movement to establish colleges on Indian reservations began, and it did as much or more to positively impact Indian education than non-Indian schools and colleges did.

The first school established was Navajo Community College in 1968, followed by Sinte Gleska College (now University) on the Rosebud Reservation and Oglala Lakota College on the Pine Ridge Reservation in the early 1970s. Now, according to the American Indian Higher Education Consortium (AIHEC), itself established as a consequence of native colleges, there are thirty-seven institutions of higher education on Indian reservations. Most are community colleges, but several are four-year schools, and some of those have graduate programs.

The significance of this ongoing phenomenon is that native people changed into a useful tool the very instrument that had been used to destroy native culture. There are two basic missions for each of those tribal institutions: to preserve native language and culture and to provide native (and other eligible) students a means of obtaining an education at home. The missions, philosophies, and staffs of those colleges are designed to meet the needs of native students and the reservation community. The establishment and success of these colleges is an achievement that was not so much as a passing thought in anyone's mind in the beginning of the boarding school era.

Beyond the issues of land, race, religion, law, and education, many other facets of native lives and cultures have been transformed as a consequence of our interaction with Europeans and Euro-Americans. Like most people, we are individually the sum of our life experiences and the choices we have made.

Although we, the current generation of native people, were not present when our ancestors signed a treaty or fought a battle or were imprisoned or made a trip to Washington, DC, such events and occurrences are part of who and what we are. Linear time is not in the equation. While many cultures and individuals regard the past as passé and as having little or no connection to the present, we do not. For example, the 2010 settlement of the lawsuit against the federal government for the mismanagement of billions of dollars of Indian monies (*Cobell v. Salazar*) is just as much a part of our cultural experience as the establishment of the BIA in 1824. The fact that the lawsuit happened is more important than when it happened. Inasmuch as the ash tree is transformed by the skills and tools of the bow maker, we natives have been transformed by these events.

We are clearly different from our ancestors in many ways because the different aspects of our individual and cultural lives have changed over time, and these changes were caused or accelerated by the arrival of European newcomers who stayed. We no longer live in direct or consistent contact with the natural environment. We no longer make our living primarily by hunting, fishing, whaling, gathering, or planting. Those of us who were nomads no longer are, and all of us live in permanent communities or villages, be they urban or rural.

Perhaps the most profound difference is the diminished role of elders in our families and communities, and most notably their absence in the leadership hierarchies. In the past, many native societies were governed by wisdom and relied on the experience and insight of elders. Modern tribal governments are just as fractionated and politicized as any form of government anywhere. Leaders are politicians and not necessarily wise people, nor do they seem to be inclined to seek the wisdom of elders.

A popular topic of conversation among some of us contemporary natives is the lifestyles of our ancestors and the kinds of skills, knowledge, and abilities they had to have in order to survive and thrive hundreds of years ago on the plains, in the ice and snow, in the forest, or in the desert. Few of us now would be able to survive and function in that environment and under those circumstances. What some of us do not discuss is the fact that a 1620 or 1750 version of our ancestors would probably not survive, much less thrive, in what the native world is today. But they would try, and so would we, if we found ourselves in 1620 or 1750. Given time, they and we might succeed. Therefore, the basic differences between us now and us then may simply be our skill sets. Other characteristics, such as motivation, will, stubbornness, courage, and compassion, may be the same.

So when we ask the question, "are we better or stronger than our ancestors?" the answer is no. We are simply different because our circumstances are different. We are probably just as aware of our specific native cultures today as they were then.

But we also face a circumstance that they did not: we must take into account what the so-called mainstream culture is and what place it has in our lives. In the final analysis, we contemporary natives are not better than our ancestors because we and they share a common reality: we must use the qualities, virtues, and values that make us uniquely who and what we are in order to survive and thrive, just as they did. We do not always succeed, and neither did they. Nonetheless, they endeavored to succeed, just as we must.

When we gaze into the pond as Iktomi did, we may be confused by what we see because our perception may be skewed by a long list of factors. Chief among them are the influence of other viewpoints, a lack of realistic cultural awareness, and an imprecise knowledge of our own history. And it may be that we do not like what we see, but we should probably accept the fact that all the images reflected in the pool are us. We are no better or worse than our ancestors, but we have been, nonetheless, transformed by the bow maker, our interaction with the newcomers who came and stayed.

What does transformation mean in our lives individually, no matter who we are?

The answer is that we are constantly faced with choices we either make or do not make. Choices made or not made lead to small or large changes. Small and large changes lead to transformation.

We can control the process of transformation as much as possible, beginning with choices. Control means making informed choices and handling as well as we can the changes we have brought about. The more control we exert, the more we can be like the bow maker who approaches the task of crafting a bow thoughtfully, skillfully, and knowledgeably.

We, as native people, became like the bow makers in control when we began to learn about the "dominant" culture and when we began to function and participate in that culture with growing awareness. It was then that we began to affect how the process affected us. That control is the primary reason we are who and what we are today—new and different with a bit of the old, not necessarily stronger or better than the original, but transformed to be equipped for and able to contend with the environment we live in today.

Therein lies the key for anyone, native or non-native, contending with transformation. I believe that no one is free from unwanted circumstances that can lead to or cause some degree of transformation in who and what we are—or perceive ourselves to be. If we are sucked into a fast-moving stream, we have two basic choices: we can succumb to the whims of the current and hope we survive until we reach a shore or calmer waters, or we can use whatever strength and ability we have to control how the current affects us.

Even for those of us who are mostly satisfied with who and what we are, transformation is still an issue. Every new day and every new circumstance or situation might transform us to a small or great degree.

Furthermore, though we may be satisfied with who and what we are, we can strive to be something better or stronger if we so choose. We do not have to wait for something or someone to affect us; we can seek to transform ourselves.

Transformation can make something positive and strong into something even more positive and stronger. Take, for example, the primitive Lakota archers. From the first moment a bow and arrows were placed in their hands, their quest was to become the best marksmen they could be. It was a lifelong quest. No less than the comfort and survival of their families and their society rested on their skills with the bow and arrow. In that instance, transformation was a continuing process.

2

Simplicity

Across the River

Among the bands who lived west of the Great Muddy River, the name Brings The Lance always evoked stories. Not so much stories of great exploits, though he was known for those as well, many of the stories of Brings The Lance were about how simply he lived, how he was a man of few words, and how he seemed to have the ability to make something out of nothing. All of that was true, but there was more to Brings The Lance.

No one, before or since, had achieved his status and reputation as a scout. Scouts were elite warriors, known for their abilities to endure hardship; to perform their missions in any weather, under any conditions; and to disappear into enemy territory for days and days. As a young warrior, Brings The Lance had returned from a scout deep into enemy territory to the north, bringing back with him the feathered lance of a well-known warrior leader from an enemy village. That was how he had earned his name. As his accomplishments grew, a few of his close friends referred to him simply as The Lance, acknowledging a daring side of the man. He would go into enemy territory armed only with a knife and a short lance.

Young warriors wanted to learn from him, so that they, too, could cultivate the art of invisibility and stealth. One day, when The Lance had reached the age when men no longer took to the warpath, a young warrior asked who had taught him to be such an accomplished scout. The Lance's answer surprised the young warrior.

"My grandmother," The Lance told him.

"How?" asked the warrior, rather skeptically.

"I took her across the river one day, when I was just a boy. My name was Little Horn then. . . . "

On a cloudy late-summer day, Little Horn gave in to his mother's plea and helped his grandmother, Grass Braid, cross the river. It had been a summer of heavy rains, so the river was higher than usual. Though he reluctantly left playing with his friends, the boy adored his grandmother and always enjoyed her company, which was unusual for most thirteen-year-old boys. As it turned out, he would never forget this particular walk across the river.

To cross it, they removed their moccasins in order to feel the rock-strewn bottom. Little Horn held his grandmother's walking stick firmly, so she could pull herself along against the strong current. In her lifetime of nearly seventy winters, the old woman had crossed many rivers, so she was not lacking in experience, only strength. With her grandson's patient assistance, she reached the far bank.

She was worried that the heavy rainfalls might have knocked down the cherries from a thick stand of chokecherry not far from the river. She had been keeping an eye on that thicket all summer, because it always yielded a lot of cherries.

After a slow trek to the chokecherry thicket, the old woman and her grandson picked a bagful of cherries. On the way back to the river crossing, the low gray clouds opened and drenched the land with a heavy rain. Little Horn led his grandmother up a slope to wait out the downpour beneath a large cottonwood tree. But Grass Braid had seen this kind of rainfall before. She knew it would not let up anytime soon.

By the time the rain did stop, it was nearly sundown, and the ground was saturated. The rain had made the ground soft and muddy and the tall grass slick. Walking was difficult.

Then they heard it, a low rumble, almost like a growl, coming out of the ground itself.

"What is that, Grandmother?" the boy asked nervously.

"A flood," she told him. "Because of the rain, creeks overflow. There is nowhere for the water to go but into the river. We should get higher up the slope, to the top of the hill, if we can."

From the hilltop, they watched the light-brown water of the river turn into a dark and swift undulating current. It was still growling like an angry beast. Driftwood, grass, and entire trees rolled in the flood.

"How will we get home?" the boy wondered.

"We wait," Grass Braid replied gently. "While there is still light, go and gather all the small, dead branches you can find on the trees. We need a fire and a place to spend the night."

"What about the village?" Little Horn was plainly worried, looking at the roaring current below them. It had not abated.

"Our village is on a flat above the bottomland," the old woman reminded her grandson. "Everyone knows about the rain. So I am certain everyone is safe. I think I can hear dogs barking. But they will be worried about us. So we must build a fire to let them know we are here, and safe, as well. There is a buffalo-berry stand just over there. We will build a shelter inside of it."

There were other worries the boy had, but he said nothing as he went to perform his task. There were animals out there, and in a while it would be dark. Bears and the big cat were his main concern. His bow and the few arrows in his quiver would be no match against either one of those creatures. He knew the other reason his grandmother wanted a fire. Animals were leery of fire and would stay away.

Running from one thicket and grove to another, Little Horn managed to gather a large pile of dead branches and twigs. None was thicker than his wrist, but there were enough to keep a small fire burning through the night.

Grass Braid, meanwhile, cleared away some of the thorny branches in the center of the buffalo-berry thicket with her knife and built a lean-to shelter. She skillfully interwove branches as a windbreak. With enough smaller, leafy branches woven in, the lean-to would even shed a bit of rain. From a distance, it was not easy to tell that the lean-to was inside the thicket.

Little Horn dug a round fire pit in front of the lean-to and started a fire. It was dusk now. The air was cool, and their clothes were still damp. Warmth was a welcome assurance.

"You might make a fire arrow," his grandmother suggested. "Shoot it high and over the river, but do not go close to the water. Someone will be looking for us and will see your arrow. They will know we are safe."

As a few stars could be seen among the breaks in the clouds, Little Horn finished his fire arrow, went down the slope, and let it loose high into the air. He could see its trail of sparks and its brief flame as it impaled the ground on the other side of the river. In a while there was an answer. Another fire arrow streaked across the sky. The people in the village knew they were safe.

Food was not a concern. They had berries, and Grass Braid had a small bag of dried meat. But there was no way to know when the river would go down. The old woman suggested it might be a few days before it was safe to cross. So there was no choice but to wait and improve their shelter, because it was certain to rain again.

Pulling out lengths of cord made from soft strips of braided hide, Grass Braid suggested that a few rabbit snares might catch something during the night. Little Horn knew about snares, so he expertly set three around a bramble thicket farther up the slope.

After that, they settled in for the night, sitting close to the low flames to dry their clothing. As he would one day be a warrior, it was Little Horn's duty to keep watch, so he did not look at the fire. That way he could easily see anything that moved in the darkness.

Morning came with a partial sun, but gray clouds still slid across the sky. Light brought a sense of relief. Little Horn climbed the hill behind them and could see the tops of the lodge poles in the village. He happily reported to his grandmother that the village was safe. One of the snares had caught a rabbit. After the boy skinned and butchered it, Grass Braid roasted it over the fire.

Sometime in the morning, they heard shouting and saw a group of men on the other side of the river, which was still running high. Little Horn saw his father among them. He went down to the shore and reassured him that he and his grandmother were safe, and that they would cross the river when the water subsided. Little Horn's father tossed a bag of food, weighted with a stone, across the water. Then he threw over a long, stone-tipped lance.

Using the daylight to good advantage, the boy and his grandmother gathered as much dry firewood as they could find. They also wove slender green branches together to extend the roof of the lean-to. The covering would keep them dry and keep the fire going. Then Little Horn watched from the top of the hill. Though he saw deer and buffalo in the distance, he saw no bears or big cats, much to his relief.

The river was still too dirty to drink. But sometime in the afternoon, the old woman recalled that there was a spring in the next little valley to the west. She was right. In the middle of a grove of oak and ash at the bottom of a gully, they found fresh water seeping out of the ground. In the soft mud, they saw vestiges of tracks washed away by the rain, so it was difficult to tell what they were. Grass Braid guessed that the spring attracted all manner of animals, from prairie dogs to bears. They filled their water flasks and hurried back to their shelter.

Little Horn kept watch from the top of the hill until the sun went down. Across the river on the far plateau, he could see the dim glow of fires where the village was. In between, the river was still deep, but it had gone down, leaving a wide swatch of debris and flattened grass on both sides.

As dusk gave way to darkness, stars could be seen between the strips of clouds. Wolves howled, a screech owl cried, and coyotes barked. Now and then came the faint whistle of a bull elk and the sudden bellow of a buffalo. Those were voices and sounds the boy had heard all of his life. But never had he felt so distant from home, even though the village was just across the river.

Grass Braid sensed his uneasiness. She knew her grandson was not afraid, but the flood cutting them off from home was a new experience for him. His father and uncles were training him to be a good hunter and warrior. The boy was learning his lessons well, but sometimes life itself stepped in with an unexpected lesson or two.

That evening she told him stories about his grandfather, her husband, who had died only three winters past. Some of the stories he had not heard before. He had not known that the long scars on the back of his grandfather's right shoulder were from an encounter with a big cat. Now he knew where his grandfather had gotten the hide, complete with head, claws, and long tail. That hide had been made into a bow case and arrow quiver. No one else had one like it.

"How did Grandfather kill the cat?" he asked.

"With a short lance," Grass Braid told her grandson. "He always carried one. The cat jumped from a tree, he said, faster than thought. All your grandfather could do was react to the motion he saw in the corner of his eye. A bow and arrow would not have been fast enough. The lance was already in his hand. Even into his old age, he carried that short lance, although it was little more than a walking stick. But he was always ready for anything, he said."

Little Horn had always been curious about the bow case and quiver that hung in his grandparents' lodge. Now he knew how and why it had come to be. He fell asleep amid images of his grandfather and a big cat.

Another night passed and gave way to a gray morning. The clouds were not as thick or low as they had been—a good sign. A warm breeze sprang up at midday and dried the land. In the afternoon, Little Horn and his grandmother climbed to the top of the hill above their thicket and sat in the sun.

"We have been on this side of the river for three days," observed the boy.

"Yes," she agreed. "Three days in your life is a long time. Three days in my life is like the blink of an eye. No matter which side of life we are, everything has a beginning and an end. In time, we will go home. I have a feeling your father has a plan."

Two more days passed, and the clouds were thinning out and retreating. The river was dropping down to its usual banks, but the current was still strong. Little Horn stood watch on the hilltop, keeping his father's lance at hand. From the buffalo-berry thicket, he heard a soft pounding. Thinking his grandmother needed help, he hurried down to see her pounding chokecherries. She had found two stones near the river, one larger than the other. The smaller she used for the hammer stone and the other, flatter one was the base. There was already a large pile of pounded chokecherries drying in the sun.

All around the edges of their thicket, Grass Braid had sprinkled a strip of cold ashes from their fire. She explained to her grandson that snakes would not crawl across dry ashes. Now that the sun was out and the land was warmer, snakes would be moving.

Just before sundown, Little Horn's father, Grass Braid's elder son, came to the river with news. Several ropes had been braided together into one long and stout cord. In the morning, two strong men would use it to cross the river and help Little Horn and his grandmother cross the water.

So Little Horn's sojourn with his grandmother in the buffalo-berry thicket came to an end the next day. So did the summer of heavy rain. It gave way to autumn, which yielded to winter. As the seasons passed, Little Horn grew closer to his grandmother. Another summer came around, and he went on his first patrols as a fledgling warrior in the company of his father and other men.

Brings The Lance gazed at the young man sitting at his fire. Like others before him, the young man was perplexed at the old scout's story.

"My grandmother taught me much in those five days," The Lance said. "All she carried across the river was her knife, an empty bag for berries, and a small bundle of dried meat. That was what I could see. What I could not see was how she approached life. Her way was simple and straightforward. That philosophy, combined with her considerable knowledge, made her a very powerful person.

"With only that knife, she was able to make a comfortable camp for us. She wove green stalks for a shelter to keep the rain off. She knew that animals like big cats and bears were hesitant to enter a buffalo-berry thicket, because of the thorns. She knew that snakes would not cross a barrier of dry ashes. These were all simple realities, and they can often be the difference between life and death.

"Before she died, I learned all I could from her. She knew she was teaching me how to live life, though she may not have known she was teaching me how to be a scout."

The young man was thoughtful for a moment. "Does that mean, Grandfather," he asked quietly, "that the more you know in your mind the less you can carry in your hand?"

The Lance smiled. "Yes. And the less you carry in your hand, the faster you can move and the better you can hide and blend in to everything around you. That is how I was able to be a good scout."

THE EFFECTIVENESS OF SIMPLICITY

Whatever else a primitive Lakota bow is perceived to be, it is simple. As a matter of fact, an arrow, which seems simpler, has more parts to it. An arrow consists of the shaft, two or three feathers, the point, and three sinew wraps to hold down the feathers and the point; it has at least seven different parts (not counting dabs of glue).

On the other hand, the bow, in its basic form, has only two components: wood and sinew string. Some bows, with sinew or rawhide backing, have three components.

Together, bow and arrows are a simple weapons system— simple, but effective.

There were three versions of the Lakota bow: the long hunting bow, the buffalo-hunting bow, and the combat or war bow. There were three versions of the arrow as well: the long hunting arrow, the short buffalo arrow, and the short arrow matched to the combat bow.

Hunting anything other than bison from horseback was a deliberate activity. Chasing bison on horses occurred only briefly in the overall history of the Lakota. Before horses, the hunter stalked game on foot or waited in ambush for it. (This hunting method was still used extensively even after the horse came.) Hunting was deliberate because it required patience, in addition to stalking, tracking, and shooting skills. This type of hunting required a long bow to help ensure success.

The long hunting bow was at least a hand's width (about four inches) longer than the war bow and sometimes more. The length of the long hunting bow came about because Lakota archers realized that a long arrow was heavier than a short one, and a heavier arrow could better penetrate an animal hide. The long hunting bow could fire a longer, heavier arrow. The limbs of the bow had to be lengthened and tillered (shaped to bend uniformly) to enable a longer draw. All of these factors enabled the hunter to take deliberate aim at a target, the vital organs of deer and elk.

After the arrival of the horse, the buffalo-hunting bow, the shortest of all the bows, was used on horseback. A short bow was easier to maneuver, especially at thirty miles an hour. It had a short, powerful draw and was the stoutest of the Lakota bow designs. Much of its power came from the layers of sinew glued to the back. It needed to be powerful because the bison had a thick hide, thick musculature, and wide ribs. The bow needed to send its arrow with enough force to slice through all that material.

The war or combat bow was the version most simply made and made in greater numbers than hunting bows. Most war bows were short, like buffalo-hunting bows, but not backed with sinew. The rationale was simple: War bows were likely to be damaged, lost, or destroyed in the chaos and confusion of combat. A plain, unbacked bow was not as great a loss as a sinew-backed hunting bow. A sinew-backed bow required nearly ten times the effort and time to make. War bows were short because, like buffalo-hunting bows, they were often used from the back of a horse. Most warriors on patrol or going into battle carried at least one spare war bow.

War arrows and buffalo-hunting arrows were similar. Both were short; sometimes the buffalo arrow was shorter, because it was shot from horseback, often when the horse was traveling at a gallop and over uneven ground. Under such conditions, a short arrow was easier to maneuver. Both kinds of short arrows had only two feathers for the fletching, and the feathers were positioned on exact opposite sides of the shaft, in line with the direction of the notch of the nock. Two feathers enabled the archer to rapidly load the arrow (place the arrow on the bow string) and fire it. Buffalo arrows were always made from hardwoods, such as the chokecherry. Hardwood shafts were heavier and more durable than softwood shafts, such as those made of willow.

Hunting arrows were also usually made of hardwood, but in addition to being longer, they had three feathers for the fletching. Three feathers (split and trimmed), each about five inches in length, placed at a slight angle on the shaft caused the arrow to spin in flight, thus enabling greater accuracy. Arrow fletching was made from any kind of feather that was available, but the craftsman used the same kind of feather (from the same kind of bird) on one arrow. A raven feather was not used with a turkey feather, for example.

For hunting arrows used in winter or damp conditions, goose and duck feathers were used, because they were naturally water repellent. Some hunters took the additional step of putting a thin coat of oil (rendered fat) on arrows to be used in the winter or in wet weather. Any kind of fat worked, but many preferred the fat from ducks and geese.

In winter or wet weather, spare bow strings were kept in heavily smoked or oiled bags to keep them dry. Wet bowstrings stretched.

Even before a tree became a bow and a thin wood stalk became an arrow, it was measured specifically for the bow-and-arrow user. The measurement was simple and sensible. The basic length of the bow was the straight diagonal distance from the tip of the archer's middle finger, with the arm outstretched horizontally, to the outer (opposite) point of the archer's hip. If it was to be a hunting bow, a hand width was added to this length, or the total length was measured as the distance from the ground to the cleft at the top of the standing man's rib cage, at the base of the throat. Buffalo-hunting and war bows were usually the length between the ground and the standing man's waist.

Most arrows were the length of the shooter's arm from the point of the bent elbow to the tip of the middle finger, plus the width of a hand (about four inches). Hunting arrows to be used with longer hunting bows were lengthened another two fingers' width.

Though the methods of measurement for bows and arrows were common, the finished bows and arrows varied in length, of course, because not all archers were the same size. To further personalize arrows, a crest was painted within the space at the nock or notch-end of the shaft the length of the feathers. That crest was a colored band or series of bands around the shaft. The same crest was used for both hunting and war arrows.

After a communal bison hunt was finished and buffalo carcasses were scattered across the prairie, women and children came to butcher the slain animals. To locate the carcasses that belonged to their family, they looked at the arrows protruding from the bison carcasses until they found the arrow crest that identified the hunter or hunters in their family.

Every aspect of the bow and arrow was reduced to its simplest possible form. The basic design and configuration of a bow made it easy to build. A simple design, a simple approach, a process with the fewest possible steps or the fewest parts ensured optimum results.

That primitive weapon system followed a philosophy that can be employed in our contemporary lives: simplicity.

A simple approach is always the best. As a law of physical science states, the closest distance between two points is a straight line.

Overall, the primitive, pre-reservation culture of the Lakota made good use of the simple approach. Simplicity was the root of every method or philosophy. This is not to say that life could not become complicated, because it often did. But the simplest way to achieve an objective or solve a problem was always preferred.

As I have written elsewhere, the early years of my childhood spent with my maternal grandparents were happy and much too brief. Though later periods and a variety of difficult and good experiences would add to who and what I am, those early years were my foundation. There were numerous lessons for me during that time, but one of the most profound was the lesson of simplicity.

This lesson was profound because simplicity worked. Keeping things simple was more than a philosophy; it had practical application day in and day out. My grandparents chose a simple lifestyle in order to make the most of the resources available to us. They also chose it because they came from a long line of people who had lived as simply as possible.

Having material riches was not important to my grandparents. Having enough to get by on and be comfortable was the goal. I cannot recall a single instance of being cold or hungry. Looking back now on my time with them, I know how they were able to provide everything we needed to be happy, healthy, clean, fed, and warm. They lived within their means.

Their monetary income was limited and fixed, and most of it came from my grandmother leasing pastureland to a neighboring rancher. A garden was plowed and planted, and we kept at least half of the harvest. A great deal of the other half was bartered for food staples—such as flour, salt, sugar, and coffee—from one of the grocery stores in town, and some of it was given to relatives.

On a few occasions, we traded for or purchased a hindquarter of beef from one of our white neighbors. Some of the meat we consumed immediately, but the bulk of it was sliced into thin strips and air-dried, to be preserved for winter food. Likewise, we dried most of the corn we harvested, as well as "wild turnips," tubers with thick skin and long roots that we dug up in late July and early August. The covering skin was removed so the bulb could dry, and bulbs were braided together by the roots. I can still see the six-foot or longer strings of wild turnips hanging on the wall. They were delicious in soups and stews.

Our supply of meat was augmented by at least one or two deer my grandfather was able to bag in the fall and winter, and rabbit was another winter delicacy. Now and then we were able to snare a few grouse as well, and in the spring and summer, we caught bullheads in the river.

We purchased some items and supplies, such as evaporated milk, hard candy, writing materials, kerosene, white gas, lamp wicks, and when necessary, a new lamp. We bought mainly the necessities we could not make or produce ourselves. Before I came to live with them as an infant, my grandparents had acquired a large cookstove and a tall, round stove for heating. They also had three draft horses, their harness, and the wagon they pulled. The wagon was our main method of transportation, though there were many times we walked.

The only sophisticated bit of technology in our house was a battery-powered radio. On the front were two round knobs and a fan-shaped face with numbers. The battery was large, about the size of a shoebox, and it fit inside in the back. Every evening, I believe at six o'clock, my grandparents would turn on the radio to listen to the news. The radio was tuned to one station and never changed: WNAX in Yankton, South Dakota. It was the only station that came in clearly, and my uncle, my mother's younger brother, was serving in the U.S. Army in Korea at the time. (For me, that broadcast was the only time I consistently heard the English language spoken. Church on Sunday did not count, because the priest did not always seem happy.) Though the news broadcast was only fifteen minutes long, there almost always was a mention of Korea. As I recall, when that conflict ended, my family heard my uncle's name among a list of local servicemen who were coming home. His letter with the same news came days later.

Living seven miles from town and three miles west of a north-south highway, we rarely had unwanted visitors, though we frequently had surprise guests. It was not unusual for one of our white neighbors to drop by. One, a bachelor farmer, was a good friend to us. But the visits we enjoyed most were those of Lakota friends and relatives. It was not unusual for some of them to spend the night or several nights.

We had no telephone, and I had no idea what one was or that such a thing existed. My grandmother would not use a telephone until 1962, and my grandfather never did.

There were other ways in which simplicity was part of our years on the plateau above the Little White River. There was little traffic on the highway east of us, and if there was, we saw it rather than heard it. Some nights we saw headlights. On clear nights, the stars were intense, and it almost seemed possible to reach up and touch them. There were certainly no satellites in the night sky and almost no airplanes, though a small one chugged by now and then in the daylight. Even more infrequently, very large planes roared overhead. My father said they were bombers from the air force base in Rapid City, to the west.

Mostly, there were the sounds of breezes and wind, birds and coyotes. We heard owls and nighthawks at night and the thud of dancing grouse in the early morning. I recall on many quiet winter mornings the muffled drumming of the horses trotting back toward the hay barn to be fed, or the ringing crack of my grandfather's axe splitting firewood. All of those sounds and more are still, for me, the symphony of a simple life—a life I find myself yearning for quite frequently these days, amid the constant noise of contemporary life, both inside the supposed sanctuary of home and outside.

I am reminded that simplicity is less hectic and less stressful. Simplicity is peace.

I wonder sometimes if we modern humans are past the salvation of simplicity. I wonder if noise and fast-paced motion and the preponderance of just plain stuff has now crept into our DNA. Somehow, I think we have become afraid of silence and stillness and the uncomplicated way of doing anything. It seems impossible for us to make a trek across town without armloads or packs full of all the things that we are convinced are necessary for our daily existence. I doubt if we would be able to go anywhere empty-handed without feeling a bit of panic. I must admit to a twinge of vulnerability whenever I forget to take a cell phone. But as soon as I do, that log house on the plateau pops into my memory, just ahead of the image of an ash-wood bow.

Such a bow hangs in my office. It reminds me that everything has a place and a purpose. Someday it will be in the hands of my youngest grandson, who is now five years old. Its purpose, among others, is to remind me of simplicity. Hopefully, I will have the opportunity to tell him about that attribute.

It also reminds me that the best years of my childhood were just that because life was basic and simple. There were certainly complicated issues and circumstances that I was not aware of at the time. My parents, for example, moved around frequently because my father went from job to job, and all of those jobs involved hard physical labor on farms and ranches. For a few years he broke horses.

The most difficult complication was an injury to my grandfather's leg, which turned into a chronic condition. His leg was the reason we had to leave the log house on the plateau and move into town. Yet even after we moved into town, my grandparents kept things as simple as possible. There were never any knickknacks in our house, nothing extraneous. Our home was pleasant and clean, adequately but not superfluously furnished. Though we had electricity, our appliances were manual can openers, hand-cranked coffee grinders, and hand-powered mixers. My grandparents were too used to doing for themselves to give in to modern conveniences. Only later did my grandmother acquiesce to an electric iron, toaster, and radio. Much later, there was a refrigerator, a wringer washer, and an electric coffee maker—things that had become basic necessities for others but still had to prove their worth to my grandmother.

I have simplicity in my pedigree.

Today, my intention is to simplify, to slow down, to find a quiet way, a quiet place. In general, it is to resurrect that part of my psyche that knows simplicity and to remember the difference between the things I want and the things I actually need.

Given how numerous and sophisticated gadgets have become, the words *adequate* and *simple* have a slightly different meaning than they once did. My wife and daughters have the latest cell phones and applications that enable them to receive e-mail on those phones. They type out texts on a keyboard so small only a gopher has fingers that fit it, and I honestly do not understand how humans can use it. I do have a cell phone, but only a basic model, one that I can understand and use.

When I was a freshman in college, the first paper I wrote for English composition was in longhand, a choice offered by the instructor if we did not have access to a typewriter. To ensure neatness, the instructor required we use a ballpoint pen. My younger children learned something called keyboarding in elementary school, and now my grandchildren are learning it, too. Now there is no longer a concern for neatness, only for which font to use.

I know it is necessary to move beyond context for me to rediscover simplicity, because context has a way of validating people, things, thoughts, and actions, no matter how stupid or useless or harmful they are, if they hang around long enough. Consequently, *simplicity* has a different meaning now than it had in the 1950s. It stands to reason then that the simplicity of the 1950s would have been regarded as much too complicated in 1900.

Therefore, here is what I think simplicity means for me today:

- Though there is an endless list of complicated things and ways and ideas, I can choose which, if any, will be part of my life this moment, today, or ever.
- Not only does the television remote let me change channels, but it also has an off button.
- While I do text and e-mail, I can let people know that I prefer to have a conversation without having to record a message or listen to one, and what I prefer most is to talk face-to-face, in person (without Skype).
- I will not do business with any establishment or company that forces me to listen to a list of recorded options.
- I may let a GPS find me if I get lost, but I will not let one tell me where to go. I have a hard time depending on something that does not have warm blood or a soul.
- I will never forget that the pencil predates the word processor and printer.
- Nor will I forget that the storyteller came before the book, that the spoken word is much older than the written word.
- Walking a thousand steps is far more beneficial to my health than driving a thousand miles.
- Silence is the path that leads to knowing myself or getting reacquainted with myself.
- Advanced age is a consequence of chronology; any wisdom that may come with old age must be earned.
- Wisdom that I have earned does not belong to me; it is available as a gift to anyone younger who truly seeks it.

- I will always be thankful for any amount of good health I have.
- I will always be grateful to wake up to a new day.
- I will approach each day knowing that those who have gone before me are watching, and those who come after me will reap what I do with that day.
- I will not let the good or the bad of the past own me, but I will let it teach me.
- I will never forget those who have helped me along the way, and I will endeavor to forgive those who tried to hinder me.
- I will never forget where I came from.
- I will never forget that I have an obligation to give happiness and that giving happiness is the way to receive it.
- Character weighs nothing, but it has a weighty impact.
- I will never forget that I came into the world with nothing.
- Living this moment and this day well is within my ability.
- All of the foregoing can be attempted and accomplished and realized and learned and remembered without a gadget or an instrument of any kind.

In chapter 1 I described a conversation among grandfathers. On that Sunday afternoon in the 1950s, the grandfathers were talking about simplicity. Their comments haunt me to this day. One of the grandfathers complained that many aspects of life had become very complicated.

There were two general characteristics that the grandfathers ascribed to white culture: loud and complicated. For example, though the automobile was superior to the horse in some ways, on the whole it had many, many parts. If just one part broke or wore out, it usually disabled the whole.

To illustrate the point further, one of the old men told the story of collecting lease money from a white rancher who leased his land. The quarter section had been leased through the BIA. Lessees were required to go to the BIA agency offices in the small town of Rosebud. That was the easiest part of the process. Once in the lease office in Rosebud, the old man had to wait until an official could see him. Then he had to prove who he was. Next a copy of the lease papers had to be verified. After that, at least two, sometimes three officials had to sign off on his request to receive his lease payment. The final step was for the check to be written. The grandfather telling the story endured this complicated process for the staggering sum of thirty dollars. Then he had to take the check to a store or a bank to cash it. This was but one example of how everything the whites did was complicated. There was nothing to be done but laugh and put up with it.

The storyteller closed his comments by telling of his own grandfather who, long ago, traded horses with another man. Each man handed the lead rope of the traded horse to the other man, and the transaction was concluded.

Life is complicated, but that does not mean we have to face it and live it in complicated ways. I recall my grandfather drawing a circle in the dirt one day—a large circle about two feet in diameter. Then he marked two straight lines through the middle, one horizontal and the other vertical.

The circle, he said, was life. The points where the two lines touched the circle divided it into four parts: birth, childhood, adulthood, and old age.

The two lines were two roads in life; one was the easy way, and one was the more difficult way. The easy way was the Black Road, and the hard way was the Red Road. The easy road was wide and flat, and at the end of it was nothing. The hard road was narrow, with twists and turns, and fraught with obstacles and losses and failures, victories and defeats, and at the end of it was strength and character.

The interesting part of that lesson was that my grandfather did not tell me which road I was to choose. He did say that it was entirely my choice. Then he followed that with another bit of advice that I have never forgotten—and I have realized the truth of it the hard way a few times.

He said, "You can think, say, and do what you want as long as you are prepared to put up with the consequences of your thoughts, words, and deeds."

In making choices in my life, I have remembered how my grandparents lived their lives. Even in the most complicated and convoluted moments and circumstances, they tried to find a simple and quiet way through it. That is probably the main reason they were two of the most emotionally grounded and spiritually centered people I will ever know in this life.

Whenever I look at the elegant simplicity and strength of a primitive Lakota bow and arrow, I think of them.

3

Purpose

The Story Keeper

Stone Bear would not say it openly to Blue Shell,
his wife, but their son Bird was something of a
disappointment to him. The boy was only twelve, but
that age was an important marker in any Lakota boy's
life, because it was on the outer edge of becoming a man.
Furthermore, every man wanted a son to follow in his
footsteps. Stone Bear was a head man in the village and
important in the Kit Fox warrior's society. Bird seemed
to be more of a thinker than a doer. Though he was
proficient with bow and arrow, he did not participate
in the usual rough-and-tumble games with other boys.
Instead, he preferred to spend time with Wasp, the old
man who was the Keeper of the Winter Count.

Bird did his share of hunting and took his turn at night
as a horse guard. There was no reason for his father to
criticize or even scold him. The boy always did what was
expected or asked of him. What puzzled Stone Bear was
that the boy would make sketches in the dirt and often sit
near a group of grandmothers or grandfathers to listen to
them tell stories. That was not the behavior of a boy who

wanted to be like his father. At Bird's age, Stone Bear had been pestering his father to accompany him on a war party.

Then one morning the situation took an unexpected turn. The Keeper of the Winter Count appeared at Stone Bear and Blue Shell's lodge. He had a request. He wanted their permission to train their son to be a story keeper. Blue Shell was honored that the wise and respected Wasp would want her son for such an important duty. Stone Bear was, too, but he was worried that Bird would never win the kind of status he himself had as a leader of warriors. The path of a story keeper was not as glorious as that of a warrior. Nevertheless, he gave his permission to Wasp. Bird was excited when his mother and father gave him the news and was eager to start learning to be a story keeper.

No one in the village was certain how old the Keeper of the Winter Count was, but since he had become the story keeper, over fifty years, or winters, had been recorded on his elk hides—he was already on the fourth hide. He had been, the elders in the village recalled, just over thirty when he had started. Wasp knew his own age, but it would have been the height of rudeness for anyone to ask him directly what it was.

The Winter Count was extremely important. In the council lodge hung several elk hides. On each hide were sketches. Each sketch depicted one singular event for one year. Most of the hides were old, and the drawings had been put down by Wasp's predecessors. Every winter, during the Moon of Frost in the Lodge, the story keeper and the old men selected the event that had been most significant for the year that had just passed. The event could be good or bad, happy or sad, and it was sketched on the Winter Count hide by the story keeper. From that one event, the story keeper could remember other things that had happened that year, or he could count back and tell someone when a particular event had occurred. For example, Wasp could count back and tell the people that fifty-seven years had passed since they had acquired horses, a few years before he became the story keeper.

People kept track of their age by how many winters they had lived, because winter was the toughest season of the year. The Winter Count was the record of the winters, or years, that had passed for the village as a whole.

It was the responsibility of the Keeper of the Winter Count to select the person who would be the next story keeper. Now and then, the new story keeper was a son or a grandson of the previous one. But Wasp had no living children, and since Bird showed a special interest in stories, everyone agreed he was the best choice.

Wasp was a wise man. He knew how Stone Bear felt about his son. So he encouraged the boy to honor the path of the warrior. There were, after all, many things in life that everyone was part of, and Wasp wanted his successor to have a wide variety of experiences. In his opinion, a storyteller had to live life in order to tell the stories properly. So Bird accompanied his father on military excursions, and he began to learn and understand the way of the warrior. Off the warpath, he continued to learn the art of story keeping and storytelling.

In order to preserve the stories, Bird had to learn how a story keeper made the sketches. The same symbols were used by all story keepers. For example, a circle with rays emanating from it represented the sun, and it was the symbol for one day. Three suns meant three days. A long horizontal line, left to right, curled upward into a diminishing circle meant a blizzard. Dots in vertical lines from the sky meant rain. The skull of a white-bellied goat (pronghorn antelope) meant drought.

Other symbols were obvious. A sketch of people moving camp, drawn showing the people moving right to left, meant they had gone west. Left to right meant they had gone east. From top to bottom meant they had gone south, and from bottom to top meant they had moved north.

A story keeper could look back at the pictures drawn by any of his predecessors and use the symbols to interpret the event depicted. But Bird also had to memorize several significant events that had occurred in Wasp's lifetime. All in all, the duties of a story keeper were not to be taken lightly, because it was through him that the history of the people was preserved.

So Bird left the days of his youth behind. He grew tall like his father and inherited his mother's infinite patience. In time he courted and won the daughter of a prominent leader of warriors. When necessary, he answered the call to defend the people against enemies and rode the path of war. And always he was a more than adequate provider as a hunter. Like most hunters, he left meat at the lodge doors of the elderly and widows.

Before Bird reached the age of twenty-five, Wasp died. With the passing of his friend, mentor, and predecessor, Bird was the only story keeper in the village.

Stone Bear and Blue Shell were proud of their son and of the granddaughter born to him and his wife, Yellow Quill. Bird had not achieved the standing as a warrior the way his father had, but everyone in the village knew that their stories were preserved by a good man who understood and honored his calling.

One day, there came shocking news. Several bearded and white-skinned men were traveling up the Muddy

River and had come to the mouth of the White
Earth River. There they had parleyed by sign with
Lakota warriors patrolling along the river. The white
men indicated they were coming to trade, and their
canoes were laden with goods.

The news spread among the Lakota villages like a fast
grass fire. White-skinned men were not unknown because
there were occasional mentions of them in some stories.
Some people thought they were real. Others thought they
were only characters in stories to frighten children, like the
two-faced giant. "If you do not listen to your mother, the
white-skinned men will get you," was a common cautionary
remark. The elders, however, knew that something as unusual
and specific as *men with white skins* could not have been made
up. They knew that just about everything in stories had its
origins in reality. Therefore, the elders advised caution where
the white-skinned traders were concerned.

Some people did not heed the elders' advice and
hurried to the White Earth River to see for themselves
how it was possible for men to have white skins and
beards. Old men from several villages invited warrior
leaders, Stone Bear among them, to a meeting. They
advised that a strong force of warriors be sent to meet the
white skins, to show them that the Lakota were strong.
The warrior leaders did as the old men advised.

One of the old men approached the story keepers from
several villages and asked them to consult their Winter
Counts to see if there was anything recorded about
white-skinned men. Bird recalled that Wasp did mention
something about such strange men. If they were in canoes,
they had probably been traveling on the big river, the
Muddy. He consulted Wasp's Winter Count hides, most of
them now rolled up and stored in the council lodge.

His search was soon rewarded. In the middle of one of Wasp's elk hides was a drawing that unmistakably depicted men—men with beards—in long, narrow canoes. Anyone with beards was not Lakota, since Lakota men had no facial hair, or at least not enough to grow long, thick beards. Bird counted back nearly forty winters. Those men with beards had come into Lakota country when Wasp had been in his prime. Above the sketch of those bearded men was a snake, the symbol for enemies. Those bearded men had not come as friends.

Also in the sketch was a long object, bent downward at one end. At the other end the object was spewing something like hailstones. Bird searched his memory, and out of the depths of the stories Wasp had told him came two words: holy iron. The holy iron, Wasp had said, was a powerful weapon that white-skinned men used, a weapon that could kill at a distance greater than bows and arrows.

Bird rolled up Wasp's Winter Count hide and rode out after his father, who was leading a contingent of warriors to meet the white-skinned men. When he reached the small village that had sprung up along the north bank of the White Earth River, he showed his father the drawings on Wasp's Winter Count. Then he told all the warriors the story his predecessor had drawn, a story that was a warning. Wasp had warned that the bearded men who had come up the river nearly forty years before were enemies, and they had carried a powerful weapon. Stone Bear did not doubt what his son the story keeper had to say. Everyone knew that it was the sacred duty of the story keepers to depict the truth. He decided, therefore, that extreme caution was the best course.

It was not long before five white-skinned men with beards were seen coming up the White Earth River.

Because it was late summer, the river was shallow and its waters were chalky white, hence its name. So the white-skinned ones were pulling three canoes, sometimes dragging them, over sandbars. As depicted in Wasp's drawings, the strangers were carrying the long weapons made of wood and iron.

Those that had come to the valley of the White Earth River would tell the story for years and years to come. They had witnessed a new kind of people coming into the territory of the Lakota. But the stories drawn on Wasp's Winter Count hide had warned that these new people may not be friends. So Stone Bear and the other warrior leaders hid their warriors among the groves of big cottonwood trees standing on either side of the river. The newcomers were obviously nervous and apprehensive, and each one of them kept his weapon in hand. When the Lakota indicated with hand signs that they were there to trade, the bearded men seemed relieved. Both sides regarded each other with great interest and acted with great caution. After dragging their laden canoes onto dry land, the strangers revealed the goods they had brought: iron knives, small iron kettles, rolls of cloth of various colors, and tiny colored seeds with holes in them (glass beads). They signed that they would trade these items for beaver skins.

The next day, there was a feast after Lakota hunters brought deer and antelope. All the white-skinned and bearded men were small, very pale, and thin. They obviously had had a long and difficult journey. There were many questions on both sides, but not all of them could be answered through the language of the hand. To a man, the Lakota warriors saw that the strangers kept their long weapons in hand. In the afternoon the strangers demonstrated their long weapons.

No doubt their intent was to instill fear—a wise move considering they were woefully outnumbered. No one, not even an experienced warrior like Stone Bear, was ready for the thunderclap voice of the holy iron. A rolling plume of white smoke from the end of the weapon was nearly as impressive. But by showing the power of their weapons, the white-skinned men also revealed a weakness. True, the holy iron had splintered a small, dead trunk at a distance of fifty paces. But to prepare the long weapon to be fired again, the man had to pour black powder into the hole at the end, then fit a round ball into the hole, push down the ball with a log rod, and pour more of the black powder onto an appendage on the other end. Stone Bear happened to count as one man did all of these things, and it had taken a long while, to the count of eighty. In that time, Stone Bear estimated that a Lakota warrior could discharge eight to ten arrows from his bow. After an arrow was released, the next could be notched on the string and released by the count of eight. Though Stone Bear was impressed by the strangers' weapons, he was not intimidated. Later that evening, he explained his observations to all the other warriors.

The next day, he invited the five strangers to a small meadow near the river. There he had several boys demonstrate their skills with the bow and arrow. Stone Bear tossed a hide ball stuffed with grass and string into the air. All of them hit it or came within a whisker of hitting it, time after time. The meaning of the demonstration was not lost on the strangers.

The strangers stayed in their camp for nearly a month. In that time, many Lakota hunters trapped and skinned many beavers, enough to trade for all the goods brought by the bearded men. One day the strangers left with their canoes loaded with beaver skins, signing that they would return again. Though the Lakota waited the next summer, the traders did not return for two years.

In the years after the Winter of the Bearded Strangers, as that time came to be known among the people who pitched their villages near the Muddy River, Stone Bear thought about their visit often. One realization came back to him again and again. If it had not been for Bird's interpretation of Wasp's warning, the people would likely have been awed by the weapons of the strangers, the holy irons. They might have been awed by something they could not understand. But the simple fact that Bird had learned that white-skinned, bearded men had come before with such weapons had prepared them for the moment at hand.

The autumn after the strangers departed, Stone Bear and Bird went hunting, after appropriate preparations under the guidance of a medicine man. Stone Bear wanted to find an elk. It was not only the meat he sought, but also the hide.

After a successful hunt, Stone Bear and Blue Shell scraped and prepared the elk hide, tanning it with a special mixture of oil and elk brains. When they were finished, they had a beautiful robe. On one side was thick, cream-colored hair, and on the other side was a soft, nearly snow-white hide. On it their son, the story keeper, would draw the pictures that would tell the stories of their people.

Bird would never stand in the lodge of the warrior societies and tell the stories of his exploits as a warrior. It was a ritual known as "telling of one's victories," and it was done by all warriors. Though Bird took to the warpath as a warrior many times, he had a different calling, a purpose. And his father realized his son had been born to honor. Bird's calling was one that would honor the people collectively. Bird was a story keeper, called to tell the stories of his people, to keep their history. It was a calling he served well into his old age, until he passed it on to his son, Stone Bear, named for his grandfather.

Among the last pictures that Bird drew on the hide given to him by his father and mother was another that told a difficult story. It was the picture of a large boat that seemed to have a square white wing. On it, and in other smaller boats that accompanied it, were more white-skinned and bearded strangers—forty of them. Like their predecessors, these bearded men also carried the long, loud, smoke-belching holy irons.

Later, long after Bird had died and some of the people learned to speak the language of the bearded strangers, they were told that the Winter of the Boat Men was known as "1804" by the white-skinned men.*

The Power of Purpose

Very few objects in the world symbolize function and purpose like a primitive bow and arrow. In fact, long ago they were used in marriage ceremonies to teach just those things.

A wise, respected old man would be asked to speak to the bride and groom and to the gathering at large. He stood before

---

*In September 1804, the Discovery Expedition, led by Meriwether Lewis and William Clark, traveled north on the Missouri (Great Muddy) River and passed through Lakota territory.

everyone, with a bow and an arrow in his hands, and talked. His words were not a lecture, but advice for the young couple and a reminder for the husbands and wives in the village. He began by telling everyone that the bow was female because it was a gift of the moon, who was a woman. The arrow was male because it came from the sun, who was a man. The function of the bow was to send off the arrow, and the function of the arrow was to fly.

But it is through the combination of their functions that the bow and the arrow find and fulfill their mutual purpose: to hit the target. The symbolism of the lesson was not lost on the audience since bows and arrows were an integral part of life in that day and age.

After he implored the young couple to be like the bow and the arrow, the old man would shoot the arrow from the bow, sending it as far as he could (often a hundred and fifty yards or more) as a visual wish for a long life together.

With the endless variety of gadgets that enters into our visual awareness in one way or another, we probably cannot at first glance (or even at fifth glance) know what each is or does. But the functions of bows and arrows, no matter what kind of bows and arrows they are (modern, traditional, or primitive; working and static recurves, longbows, reflex/deflex, compounds, or crossbows) are universally known. Even nonarchers know the functions of a bow and arrow: the bow sends the arrow, and the arrow flies.

Sadly, however, we modern humans have stripped the bow and arrow of all the meaning they started out with. Now they are superficial, inanimate objects. In the developed world, the purpose of today's bows is at least twofold: they are sold for either target shooting or hunting. Archery is an Olympic sport, and many archers compete professionally in tournaments throughout the world. Archery hunting, or bow hunting, is a popular and growing sport the world over. Overall, archery is a billion-dollar industry.

The only place truly primitive bows and arrows are still being made and used is in the remote jungles of the Amazon basin and wherever else primitive societies may still survive. The wise old man of long ago was right: function is different from purpose.

Like bows and arrows, each of us has different kinds of functions that are primarily connected to the job we have or to what we are trained for or have learned how to do. Jobs and functions change, however. In my life, so far, I have been a teacher, laborer, roofer, program administrator, proposal writer, political aide, and government liaison, among other things. Where in all of that is a purpose?

Like most people, I took a job to earn a living for my family. I did the job to help my employer fulfill its objectives and overall mission. If there was a larger purpose to my taking the job, it was probably to fulfill the cultural and societal expectation that a man has to be a good provider and a contributing member of the community.

While my purposes can and did change with each job, each of those purposes was connected to all the facets of who and what I am.

I am now a writer, but I am also an archer. As a matter of fact, I have been an archer longer than I have been a writer. As an archer, I practice frequently for two primary reasons or purposes. First, I practice for the sheer joy of it, and there is nothing like joy and satisfaction to validate anything. Second, I practice to get better as a marksman. Becoming a better marksman has been my ongoing purpose and pursuit (off and on) for sixty years. But my purposes as an archer do not end there. My primary shooting style is primitive Lakota, which uses a floating anchor and a short draw. Most archers have used an anchor point—meaning that they draw the arrow (pull the bow string back) and touch a point, be it the side of the mouth or the chin. This means they need to pull the string back to the full length of the arrow. The predominant Lakota method does not use an anchor point (floating anchor) or draw to the length of the arrow. Therefore, my third purpose is to preserve a little-known aspect of Lakota culture and history.

There is no end to our purposes. And if we choose, we can find them.

The question some of us ask ourselves is, how do I discover my purpose, what I was put on earth to do? For example, I am frequently asked the question, why did you become a writer? How did I discover that my purpose was writing? The answer begins with my grandparents, as most things in life for me still do.

My grandparents taught me a lot through stories. Family history, events, situations, dilemmas—all had a lesson. Most of the time that lesson was conveyed intentionally, but sometimes it came through unintentionally. For example, my grandmother told me about her younger sister, Fannie, who died of influenza at the age of eighteen. Fannie lingered for weeks before she succumbed to the illness, and my grandmother described her sister's strength of spirit and sense of peace at the end. She described little details, like Fannie being so grateful for every spoonful of soup and, toward the end, taking food only to please my grandmother. The story was about Fannie, but my grandmother was indirectly and unintentionally revealing something of herself: her devotion to her sister. She was Fannie's nurse and caregiver, virtually never leaving her side and then sitting by her grave for days.

As a teenager, I realized the power of stories. Furthermore, I saw firsthand how skillfully both of my grandparents told stories. I wanted to be like them (and still do), and I wanted to be able to tell stories like they did. Although it did cross my mind now and then, I never had the nerve to ask them to teach me to be a storyteller. As it turned out, teaching was not necessary. They were consistently showing me how. All the how-to was there—the tone, gestures, emotion, detail, knowledge, and delivery. But they were not the only storytellers I knew. There was an entire community of storytellers around me, including my grandparents' friends and relatives, many of whom we had fairly regular contact with. Social occasions and friends and family coming to visit us, or we visiting them, enabled that contact. And each of those occasions meant stories being told. Stories were my books and television.

My desire to be a storyteller was somewhat detoured because I started school, and like generations of Lakota children before me, I was inundated with the ways and ethnocentric attitudes of an outside culture I knew very little about. The most consistent piece of information my grandparents told me about white people was that they were in control. I began to understand what that meant in practical terms the day I started school at a government boarding and day school. In order for me to go to school, I was taken to my paternal grandparents, who lived on the Pine Ridge Reservation. The most fortunate part of that situation (in addition to spending time with them) was that they lived only three miles from the school, so it was not necessary for me to board at the school dormitory. My aunt, the youngest of Grandma and Grandpa Marshall's daughters, was still in school, and she and I rode the school bus together every day.

The daily routine of school had nothing to do with stories. It had more to do with following rules and standing in line, it seemed to me. Perhaps I am oversimplifying it a bit, but only because those two years were largely unpleasant. After two years at the government day school, I went back to the Rosebud Reservation and attended public school.

Somewhere in the later elementary years I became an avid reader, and I was reconnected to stories. One of the first novels

I thoroughly enjoyed was based on the life of Jim Bowie, the inventor of the bowie knife. The title of the book was *The Iron Mistress*. It was a fascinating story and much more interesting than "Goldilocks and the Three Bears" or "Little Red Riding Hood" and others in that category. I read those stories because I had to, but I read the novel because I wanted to. It taught me a very important thing: there was another way to tell stories—by writing them.

I was never concerned with making good grades in high school, only with making passing grades in order to graduate. But there was something that stirred within me and probably validated formal education in some way: the stories from my childhood and how the old men and women of my youth told them were always the standard to which I held anything that came to me in writing, especially history, and specifically as it related to Indians and the Lakota. The absolute arrogance and sense of impunity with which history writers talked about Indians hurt and angered me. To them, we were obstacles to be overcome and conquered, like rivers, deserts, and mountains. I was especially taken aback to see the lands where my ancestors had lived and thrived for so long called an empty place, the "Great American Desert." There, historians wrote, was "land for the taking." Somewhere inside of me was the thought that there had to be a way to tell that history better and tell the truth. In such moments, I came to a small but conscious decision to be a writer.

A first grain of encouragement came in freshman English composition at the university. The assignment was to write about an experience from childhood. I chose the day I had observed a bobcat in the thicket near the Little White River. The paper came back with corrections to my punctuation and sentence structure, but also with a note at the bottom: "Interesting story." Those words fanned a little spark of "what if." It was not yet ready to burst into even a little flame, but neither would it ever be completely extinguished after that.

In the years after that, life took me in some interesting and difficult directions, both geographically and experientially. Eventually, time was occupied with making a living and raising a family. The only obvious writing I did was lesson planning as a teacher, composing material for a course for which there was no textbook, and various letters, memorandums, and narrative reports for several nonteaching jobs. But through it all, I secretly wrote vignettes, short stories, and brief essays on whatever was an issue at the moment, such as the American Indian Movement and the 1973 occupation of Wounded Knee. "Secretly" means that I did not share these pieces with anyone else. But the desire to write meaningful stories was growing.

The first piece I published was an essay for a monthly column for the *Casper Star-Tribune* in Casper, Wyoming, in 1990. Several columns followed, and these eventually became the basis for my second book in 1995, entitled *On Behalf of the Wolf and First Peoples*. I had already coauthored a book on the Battle of the Little Bighorn in 1992.

One of the first reactions I had when I laid eyes on that first column was a sense of accomplishment. A split second behind was the realization that I had found my purpose in life.

Our purposes form from or rise out of the kind of people we are, what our values are, and where and how those purposes can fit into the world around us. No matter who we are, as children we are guided and/or influenced by the adults in our lives. When I was a child, the primary adults in my life were my grandparents. My maternal grandparents were easily the greatest influence on me, but my paternal grandparents were sources of knowledge, wisdom, and inspiration as well. My parents also had a part in the process, and my mother, who turned eighty-three years old in 2011, still does. Each of them is a story and each of them had stories to tell. And each of them was connected with the past. Fortunately for me, they all helped me find my purpose.

I believe that all of us are put on this earth to fulfill a purpose—or purposes—if we choose. Amusingly or sadly, some of us serve as examples of how *not* to do something, even if we do not consciously make that choice. I believe that my purpose, at least one of them, is to create awareness about native people. No one person can tell all of the stories, reveal all the realities, because there is so much to do. But I can be one perspective, one voice speaking from one identity, one heritage.

The most empowering aspect of this purpose—this destiny, if you will—is that it did not begin with me. I and people like me come from a long line of storytellers. In the modern era, that line began with people like Charles Eastman (1858–1939), a Dakota and one of the first Western-trained native physicians. He witnessed the aftermath of Wounded Knee in 1890 and later wrote *Indian Boyhood*, among other works. Luther Standing Bear, a Lakota and a graduate of the Carlisle Indian Industrial School, published *Land of the Spotted Eagle*, the first of four books, in 1928. A more recent writer was Vine Deloria, Jr., a Lakota from the Standing Rock Reservation. In addition to being a prolific writer, he was a theologian, a lawyer, and a wise man. Sadly, he passed away in 2005.

I do not purport to have their status, nor do I endeavor to. But I am honored to help continue the line. That is what I was put on this earth to do, as well as perhaps to inspire someone else to follow. Two of my daughters write, although they are pursuing other career paths. One is a poet with thoughts of writing screenplays, and the other likes short stories. And the next generation is already waiting in the wings. One of my granddaughters, an eighth grader, has decided that she will be a writer.

Whatever they decide to do, I know they will find a purpose, or it will find them.

HONORING PURPOSE

My grandparents and other elders in the community told me often, and gently, to remember the stories. None of them ever told me that I had to be a storyteller. I came to my own decision as a young adult after a persistent but hazy question finally came clear to me one day.

Who will pass on the stories?

I decided that I could do that—not for any grandiose reasons, ulterior motives, or recognition. I decided to pass on the stories because someone had to. That is not to say that I am the only Lakota passing on Lakota stories, because I am not.

It is critical that the core of our Lakota culture be preserved by any Lakota who has the knowledge, not primarily so that the world can receive it, but so that the information is available to the next Lakota generation.

It is imperative, however, that cultural knowledge and history be told by Lakota historians. This work is critical now because the mechanisms by which oral tradition perpetuated itself no longer function the way they once did. There is not an abundance of Keepers of the Winter Count or genuine storytellers, and there has not been for many generations. Therefore, contemporary Lakota (and Dakota and Nakota) writers, artists, singers, and dancers who preserve our history and culture in any way are now our Keepers of the Winter Count and storytellers. Most or all of those kinds of people probably consider preserving and sharing Lakota culture to be their destiny.

Destiny as a guide to purpose should not be ignored. Considering the circumstances on every reservation in South Dakota in the 1950s, many Lakota elders must have been more than a little concerned for the future Lakota culture, customs, traditions, religion, and language. The policy of assimilation was alive and, unfortunately, doing very well in all the government and parochial schools, as well as in many public schools. Missionaries were having their way and having a heyday "saving" Lakota souls. Lakota culture was slowly being diluted, decimated, prohibited, and replaced.

But the elders who were around during my childhood in the northern part of the Rosebud Reservation, and in and near Kyle on the Pine Ridge Reservation, were fighting back in their own way; they were telling stories to anyone who would listen, but especially to young people. They were telling stories to those of us who were of the next generation. As much as the boarding schools and churches tried to take our culture from us, those elders were doing their best to keep as much of it intact as possible. For the most part, they did not intentionally denigrate or ridicule the white culture, in spite of how they really felt. Instead, they told stories to present their own culture in a good and truthful light. In doing so, they taught us who we were. They taught us that it was a good thing to be Lakota, no matter what the whites were saying. They gave us a sense of identity.

There were those of us who heard the stories and took them to heart, but our sense of identity did not manifest itself in all of us in the same way. Some became singers and dancers, preserving the old songs and dances for the next generation. Many quietly conducted Lakota religious ceremonies. All of us spoke English because we had to, but we also spoke Lakota to keep it alive. And some of us became storytellers.

In a real way, those elders who told the stories, sang the songs, danced the dances, and kept the ceremonies and traditions alive shaped the destiny of those who would take up the mantle of heritage to do what we could to pass it on. They perhaps revealed our destinies and in doing so, gave us our purpose.

I still remember that cold January or February night when my grandfather and I walked down into the gully to cut the ash tree from which to craft a bow. The tree was about to meet its destiny, which was assured the moment my grandfather selected it and marked it some months earlier. Like that tree, I seem to have been selected for a specific destiny.

Somewhere in my midtwenties, a realization fell into place for me, not unlike the final piece of a puzzle, and initially it seemed rather daunting. I realized that my grandparents and all the other elders who told me stories had also been offering me a responsibility. They did not ask me or tell me in so many words, when I was a child, that I should be a storyteller. They wanted to, but they understood, because they were elders, that one day I very well could come to that realization on my own. And if after that I chose to take the offer, it would be a commitment freely taken, not a duty taken on out of a sense of obligation.

I did take the offer freely, not knowing what the consequences would be or where it would take me. It would be another fourteen years before I put everything else aside—including a challenging job with a lucrative salary—to take the first active steps to honor that responsibility and fulfill my purpose.

There are two clear rewards for knowing what our purpose in life is. First, there is the sense of fulfillment, and second, there is knowing the impact our purpose can have.

For the overwhelming majority of us, finding and fulfilling our purpose will never, ever garner us a fortune, and we will never come close to having our fifteen minutes of fame. But if we follow our purpose for fortune and fame, our motivation is suspect. Fortunately, there are people who strive to serve the greater good, toiling day in and day out for the welfare and benefit of others, including teachers, health-care providers,

social workers, emergency responders, search-and-rescue workers—those who are truly altruistic.

I am reminded of the words spoken to Lakota Shirt Men long
ago. They were young men in the community whose exceptional character and noteworthy accomplishments set them
apart. Being selected by the elders to be Shirt Men was not
a reward, but a responsibility. They were responsible for living
an exemplary life. Not all young men selected to be Shirt Men
accepted. At a public ceremony, those who did were given an
exquisitely decorated tanned-hide shirt depicting their accomplishments; hence the designation. Then an elder spoke to the
selectees. A significant part of the statement focused on what
should be done for others:

> *You must help others before you think of yourselves. Help*
> *the widows and those who have little to wear and to eat and*
> *who have no one to speak for them.*

In other words, selfish and self-centered people need not apply.

In the interest of full disclosure, I must say that the selec-
tion of Shirt Men was not untouched by politics. Sometimes
the elders were influenced to select young men from prominent and influential families, to help those families gather
or solidify political power. For the most part, however, truly
exceptional young men were picked. Among them was Tasunke
Witko, known to us now as Crazy Horse. He was included in
the last known Shirt Man ceremony among the Lakota, which
occurred in 1865.

Crazy Horse was in his early twenties. He reluctantly
accepted the honor, but in reality, he was already living
according to all the precepts set forth for Shirt Men, especially
the words above. As a teenager, he had already demonstrated
concern for those who were less fortunate. He would hunt

and bring home fresh meat for the elderly and widows. Later in his life, he gave away horses to those who needed them, so his personal herd was never very large. After he was married, he and his wife consistently provided food and other necessities, such as hides and household items, to those in need. Consequently, their lodge was always sparsely furnished and their food containers empty.

Perhaps it was Crazy Horse's destiny to answer the call of the Shirt Men in a time when the Lakota people needed inspirational leadership. He certainly did leave an unmatched legacy as an effective military leader. But he also never wavered from his concern for "those who have little to wear and to eat and who have no one to speak for them." For me, that is the more meaningful legacy of Crazy Horse and the one that reveals who he really was.

The culture that produced Crazy Horse was not based on materialism, and it taught that doing for others and giving was the right thing to do. Another set of beliefs teaches that "it is better to give than to receive." Cultures the world over espouse generosity and compassion in one way or another, because those kinds of beliefs rise out of a sense of connection and caring. I believe that the people who feel that connection—no matter their race, creed, or color—are the kind of people who make an effort to serve the greater good. Those are the kind of people whose sense of purpose makes a positive difference in the world. Their names or their deeds will never make the headlines, or at least not often enough, but they will continue to fulfill their purpose.

All too frequently, the airwaves are filled with sensational news from the sports and entertainment worlds, about the latest escapade of an athlete or performer. That news can be anything from attempted rape to drug abuse. This kind of news is broadcast because it is good for television ratings, and unfortunately, there is an audience that eats it up. Intentionally or not, the consequence of repeated broadcasts and endless interviews and "expert" commentary is that the culprits and their escapades become examples. One downside is that no matter who criticizes the culprit or how many times, the fact that he or she is on national television bestows on the person a certain amount of validation. This is especially true when the celebrity in question gets off with a light sentence or does not face any penalty or punishment.

Not as bad, but certainly within the realm of ridiculous, are the professional athletes who complain that they or their teams "get no respect." This from people who have more money than 90 percent of the people who hear their rants will ever have and who have no inkling of what real life is all about. Nevertheless, they and their issues are validated when the television reports their comments as "important" news.

I also recall a recent interview with one of the stars of the television series *Dallas* from the 1980s. He was asked what he was thinking when he saw the worldwide reaction to one season's cliffhanger scene. His almost instantaneous response was "Money!" It is possible, perhaps even probable, that he does care about his fellow man and gives some of his extremely lucrative salary and investments to charities. But in that one moment, he was the poster child of greed.

All of the foregoing are examples of people who have no sense of purpose, except perhaps to take advantage of who and what they are to garner publicity and as much money as they can make.

However, there are also celebrities in entertainment and professional sports who have a sense of compassion. Several years ago, a well-known professional baseball player (who has since retired) demonstrated that there is more to life than fame and fortune. For several years (and perhaps still), he chartered a jet airliner and filled it with underprivileged children from the city where he played. He took them to Walt Disney World, paying for their meals and lodging and giving them the adventure of their young lives. Thankfully, he is not alone. There are other professional athletes who do good works in their communities.

Then there is the movie star who endeavors to call attention to the horrific consequences—rape, genocide, and starving children among them—of a civil war in Africa, when this collateral damage does not warrant the same news coverage as millionaire athletes crying about their lots in life.

Fortunately, among those who are much more privileged than most of us will ever be are some who have found a purpose that counts; they can use their celebrity to call attention to devastating global social issues, such as poverty, hunger, ignorance, racism, genocide, disease, and homelessness, among many others.

There are serious issues that millions of people deal with and work to eliminate, improve, or mitigate every day. The names of those people and their efforts will rarely be seen in any kind of headline. But that does not stop them, because their efforts and their commitment and the outcome they work for are much more important. I think it is these kinds of people who should be on television, so that millions of other people can learn about what they do, so that others can see the face of someone who is honoring a purpose that will make a difference. Because, when all is said and done, a sense of purpose is more powerful than money. That is the reality of the real world beyond the marquee lights and box scores.

Crazy Horse accepted the shirt because he felt it was his purpose, whether he wanted the responsibility that came with it or not. Once he took the shirt, he endeavored to live his life the best way he knew how, as an example for others. In fulfilling his purpose, he achieved his destiny: being of selfless service to others. He knew he was not to seek reward and recognition for anything he did on behalf of others, and he never did. Even without reward or recognition, he had a sense of fulfillment.

Then there is the story of the blind arrow maker, a man who had lost his sight as a child. With the support of his family and community, he learned to take care of himself, and in time, it seemed to those who did not know his circumstance that he was not blind at all. Furthermore, he developed one skill that no others could match: with his sense of touch alone, he could straighten a thin green stalk of willow into an absolutely straight arrow shaft.

Men came to watch him work as he deftly stripped the bark from a green stalk and then compressed it to a uniform width from end to end by sliding it through an arrow sizer— a stone or an antler with a small, round hole in it. Then he would slowly dry the shaft over a small fire, feeling the shaft with his fingertips and straightening any bends or curves in it as it dried. When he finished each shaft, it was absolutely straight and ready for feathers and a point to be attached.

Over the years, people discussed if it was blindness that had led the man to develop such skill as an arrow maker, or if he would have had the same skill if he could see. Whatever the reason for his skill, men would offer one horse for twenty arrow shafts made by the blind man, because each of the shafts always flew straight and true. But the man never traded for his arrows, though he very likely could have had the largest horse herd in the village. He gave away each one as a gift.

Furthermore, the blind man insisted that his arrows be used only for hunting. One day, a young man asked him why.

"In that way," the blind man replied, "you and I will feed your family—you by shooting the arrow, and me by making it. Together, we fulfill a purpose."

4

Strength

Stone Knives

Nothing ever stays the same, but paradoxically, very few things change completely. There is always something remaining of the original.

In 1908, Henry One Bull came home from the Carlisle Indian Industrial School dressed in a brown wool suit, white shirt, stiff brown shoes, and with short hair. He was eighteen and proud that he had learned to be a tinsmith. Imagine his surprise when his father, a tall, proud, and dignified veteran of the Battle of the Little Bighorn, broke down and wept when he laid eyes on his only son.

The day Henry One Bull came home from Carlisle was the day Jacob One Bull decided he had to win the most important battle he would fight: the battle against his people being changed into imitations of white people. He realized what the whites—those people he still thought of as Long Knives—fully intended to do. Jacob One Bull was determined to defeat them, to take back his son. He just did not know how to go about it.

Young Henry had been called Spotted Hawk when he was taken away from his family. If the boy went, his sister could stay, the white people from the Indian Bureau said. It galled his father to have to make a bargain with the whites, but the consolation for One Bull and his wife was that their daughter would be only forty miles from home, at the school the Black Robes (Catholic priests) operated. The boy was going to a place farther than his father had ever traveled in his life. Nonetheless, the bargain was struck, and the boy was taken to the train station.

When Spotted Hawk had stepped onto that train, he was dressed in the finest tanned buckskin clothes his mother could make, and his hair hung in two braids down to his waist. He was a frightened but proud Lakota boy. Hard telling exactly what he was when he came back, especially when the first words One Bull heard him speak were in the white man's language. That was the reason he wept, because his son was more like a white man than a Lakota.

Some things had to change, and One Bull had acquiesced to many of those changes. Transportation was by foot or by horse-drawn buggy or wagon. Buggies and wagons were good, but One Bull preferred to ride his horse. He had four horses, three trained to pull the wagon and the fourth for riding. His wife had talked him into going to the Black Robe church, at least for the sake of appearances. The Black Robes had performed some kind of a water ceremony and given him the white name Jacob. His wife had become Alice and his daughter, Esther. So he was not surprised when, after two years at Carlisle, the boy had written a letter home using the name Henry One Bull.

Houses were another necessary change. When there were no more buffalo hides for lodge coverings, people used canvas. Now log houses were popular. One Bull and others around the reservation pitched tattered lodges in good weather, however. He slept in the cramped log house only in the winter.

The biggest source of annoyance was that very little about how One Bull and his family lived resembled the old ways. Nothing was round anymore. Houses were square, and so were windows, and the wagons were long squares. Even the boxes in which his wife put their food were square. They slept on above-the-floor beds, also long squares. Papers on which the whites wrote their signs and words were square as well. At least the wagon wheels were round. Something inside of him prompted One Bull to put a circle of fence posts around his square log house. He did not have any wire or log rails to finish the fence, but that did not matter. He simply wanted a circle around his house.

Everything the family used every day were things made by the whites—cups, plates, knives, kettles, skillets, axes, lanterns, stoves, and even the needles Alice sewed with. Clothing was wool or calico or cotton. One Bull made his own moccasins, however. Hard-side shoes made his feet sore.

He also made a bow and arrows to hunt with. Many times he would walk down to the gully below the house, where no one could see him, just to shoot his bow and arrows. That simple activity gave him a sense of peace, a sense that something was still like it used to be.

There was one other thing. Inside a cleverly disguised hole, beneath a dead tree stump, he hid his black stone pipe, its ash stem, its bag decorated with dyed porcupine quills, and a supply of tobacco. His wife and daughter knew he had the pipe, but he did not tell them where it was hidden. That had nothing to do with trust. The Black Robes, with the help of the Metal Breasts—the Lakotas who worked as policemen for the whites—confiscated such things. Now and then there was word that another sweat lodge had been found and burned. Sometimes medicine men were put in jail. He knew that the Black Robe at the mission had asked his wife if her husband had a pipe. She answered, truthfully, that she had not seen him use a pipe for years and years.

One Bull did pray with his pipe, mostly on days when his wife and daughter were not home. He would take his pipe to the top of a hill, from where he could see a prairie dog approaching. There, he had cleared a space inside a thicket. He also took part in sweat lodge ceremonies, which never happened in the same place twice. It was the only way to stay one step ahead of the Metal Breasts.

It was to this world and to these circumstances that Henry One Bull returned, more white than Lakota. Almost immediately he was offered work at the Black Robes' mission, since he was a tinsmith. Unbeknownst to his father, the head men at Carlisle had been writing to the Black Robes at the mission, extolling young Henry's skills and hard work. Furthermore, the father superior was quick to swoop in and employ Henry for his own reason. Henry's father, Jacob, was well known for his resistance to Christianity, albeit a quiet and unobtrusive resistance. Though the older One Bull did attend Sunday mass, the father superior knew it was only as an escort for his wife and daughter. There was talk among the more stubborn elements of the older Lakota: One Bull would never change. Therefore, any opportunity to show any fence-sitters in the Lakota community the virtue of the new ways, especially embodied in One Bull's only son, was too good to pass up. To sweeten the pot, the father superior gave Henry the use of a horse and buggy.

Henry worked six days at the mission, leaving shortly after sunup and getting home just before sundown during the summer and well after the sun went down in the winter. On the seventh day, the day the Black Robes called the "holy day," the boy went to mass, taking his mother and sister in his buggy. One Bull saddled his horse and rode along.

The boy quickly fell back into conversing in Lakota with his parents, though One Bull frequently overhead his son and daughter talking in the white man's language—English, they called it. For five years the boy had been in the east, at the place called Carlisle. Many other children and young people from the reservation had been sent there. Sadly, a few had died there, and of those who returned home, like Henry, many only barely resembled what they had been before. In essence, part of them died as well, as far as One Bull was concerned. Whether it was possible to resurrect that part was the question.

One evening One Bull was helping his friend, the medicine man Fork Tail (or Swallow), dismantle a sweat lodge, so they could hide it. The conversation, as it often did, turned to their sadness and frustration about what was happening to the younger generation. The whites and the Black Robes could not change the parents and grandparents, so they went after the children. And they went to any length to accomplish their purpose. There were too many stories of the Black Robes' harsh methods of punishment at the mission schools—stories that made the blood of fathers boil with anger. One man had challenged a Black Robe at the mission to fight him instead of spanking his daughter. The Black Robe had run and hidden, but not long after that the Metal Breasts had gone to the man's house and taken him away to jail.

"I had a dream not long ago," Fork Tail said to his old friend. "I saw a young Lakota man, very tall and very strong looking. He was walking along a strange road, black and hard. I have never seen such a road. We met on that road, and he spoke to me. He said, 'I am Lakota' in the white man's language. He wore a long, brown overcoat like some white men wear over their clothes. He opened his coat, and I heard a drum and a Lakota voice singing a song—a gathering-the-spirits song. Then he closed his coat and went on his way."

"What does the dream mean, cousin?" asked One Bull.

"It means that we Lakota will change on the outside. That is nothing new; that is part of life that has been a reality since before the Long Knives came. Things on the outside change. Once our lodges were small because they were hauled by dogs. When the horse came, the lodges became larger because the horse could haul bigger loads. Such a change did not change us as a people.

"Our children and grandchildren will learn and use the white man's language. Our clothing will be different. So, too, our houses. But inside, in our hearts and minds and spirits, that part of us can still be Lakota. It is a choice that each one of us must make. The road in my dream is the new road we are on. It is different. Some of us will keep what we are and walk it as Lakota. Those of our children and grandchildren who choose of their own free will to remain Lakota will be the strongest. It will not matter what the Black Robes or any whites say or do to them. Those will be like the young man in my dream.

"Some of us will be Lakota only on the outside. Some will turn away completely to forsake what they are, and others will only be pretenders."

It was a chilling prediction, but One Bull understood. There would be losses, but the Lakota would somehow preserve what made them Lakota. He just feared that two of the losses would be his son and daughter.

A month later a friend came with bad news. Fork Tail had been taken to jail. The Black Robes had complained loud and long to the head white man at the government agency, so the Metal Breasts had been sent out. They went to his house in the night, which was their way, and took him. For One Bull, it was not unexpected news. He and Fork Tail had talked about that possibility many times. The medicine man had said often that if the Metal Breasts did take him away, no one was to do or say anything. Anyone who reacted in word or deed would immediately be suspect. In spite of his anger and worry, One Bull did as his old friend wanted. But late one night, he did go to visit Fork Tail's wife and son. They told him that Fork Tail had been taken away from the jail. The whites at the agency would not say where. As a matter of fact, the medicine man was never seen again.

It was a difficult thing for One Bull to live with. If he ever hated anyone or anything in his life, it was the Black Robes. Yet he still accompanied his family to the church. He smiled and nodded at the Black Robes. He shook the hand of the one he knew had sent the Metal Breasts after Fork Tail, though he wanted to strangle him. Back at home he burnt sweet grass and smudged his hand, to purge any vestige of the Black Robe's touch.

One Bull realized that Fork Tail's dream carried another message: that the efforts of the whites to destroy the ways of the Lakota was an ongoing war, one that would be waged against each new generation. So it would be up to each generation to survive in order to pass on as much as possible to the next. And it had to be done quietly, even secretly.

There was another reality. One Bull knew that he could not undo with words, no matter how angry or righteous or true, what the whites had done to his son.

Thereafter, he simply went about the business of living life on the new road Fork Tail had seen in his dream. In the spring, he plowed the meadow near his house and planted the seeds the agency provided. Every month, he went to the issue station to get his family's ration of meat, beans, rice, coffee, and sugar. Late summers would find him gathering and piling wood for the stove. In the fall, he and his family harvested. In the autumn and during the winter, he took his bow and arrows and hunted the river and creek bottoms, often coming home with deer.

From the trading post he bought kerosene for the lamps, and cloth, needles, and beads for his wife and daughter. In every way, One Bull and his family were like most others on the reservation. They were dutifully living in the ways expected of them by the whites. But no one could see into the heart and mind of One Bull. No one could see him pray with his pipe on the hill, sometimes at night. What was on the outside did not matter to him. A square log house or an iron kettle or even the fact that his children spoke the white man's language did not matter. One Bull looked at the world through Lakota eyes. He measured what he saw with the values he learned from his mother and father. What he learned from them would enable him to live and die a Lakota.

One evening, Henry came home from the mission to find his father sitting by the outside fire, his attention focused on something in his hands. One Bull was carving a horn spoon. The horn was one he had taken from one of the government cattle he had helped to butcher at the issue station. Henry was intrigued. As a tinsmith, he was an artisan, but he had forgotten that his father was as well. Making a spoon from horn was unique.

"My father taught me to do this," One Bull pointed out. "He learned it from his father. In the old days, spoons, cups, and ladles were made from buffalo horn. But those longhorn cattle from the issue house are good for something, other than stringy meat."

"Can you teach me?" Henry asked.

"Yes. First we boil the horn to soften it."

After several evenings, they made three more spoons, and from each of the remaining ends, One Bull fashioned cups. Henry was amazed.

That was how it began, the undoing of Carlisle.

Henry began to see his father in a different light— through the eyes of a young man beginning to question the words, thoughts, and ideas that had been thrown at him for five years. As a thirteen-year-old boy he had not given much thought to what kind of man his father was. He did remember being somewhat afraid of his father. There seemed to be something more to the man than what he could see and hear. It was almost as if something, or some part of his father, was waiting, or perhaps hiding. Henry knew that his father had been at the Greasy Grass Fight. His mother had told him, and she also warned him never to ask about it. Perhaps that was it, but Henry sensed it was something more.

The answer revealed itself the day he brought home a large spoon he had made in the workshop and gave it to his mother. He gave his father a butcher knife. Henry was astonished when, in response, One Bull opened a rawhide case and unwrapped a knife. Its handle was ash wood and the blade was of a shiny black stone.

"Where did you get this?" the boy asked.

"My grandfather's grandfather made it," One Bull told him, "in the days before the first white man set foot on our lands. I know of no one today who knows how to make knives out of stone. This is who we once were."

"Can you make a knife out of stone, Father?" the boy asked.

"Yes. My father taught me. But it is not easy to find this kind of stone."

"I know where there is stone like this," Henry said. "At the mission. The Black Robes have two large pieces. They are kept in a dust-covered box. I saw them one day. Perhaps I can trade something for one. If I can, will you teach me?"

"I will, for your word to teach your own son."

So it was. The Black Robes at the mission could not remember where the shiny black stones had come from. They were of no use, and the Black Robes were glad to give them away.

First, One Bull had to find the tools his father had used. One was like a hammer, made out of the heavy base of an elk antler. The others were made from the tips of deer horns. One evening, by the light of a roaring fire, One Bull studied the grain of the stone and struck it with the hammer tool. He struck it several times, each time knocking off a flat piece, until he was satisfied. The pieces were like glass, and One Bull explained that in the old days, young Lakota men made journeys deep into the Shining (Big Horn) Mountains. There, they dug out pieces of the shiny stone from a mountainside.

Henry carefully watched everything his father did, even as he absorbed the stories. It did not take long for One Bull to relearn the skill of making a stone knife. Neither did it take long for Henry to learn the basic steps. As the days and weeks went by, he became better and better. But he also yearned for the stories.

Autumn came and passed. As did winter. Henry devoted as much time as he could to refining the skill he had learned. Perhaps he did so because of the stories, which took him back to the time of the Lakota before the whites came—stories of their ancestors and how they lived. Yet every Sunday, Henry harnessed his horse to the buggy and took his mother and sister to the Black Robe church, and One Bull rode along. They honored the Black Robe ceremonies by sitting, standing, and kneeling whenever the small bells were rung. They listened respectfully to the Black Robe conducting the ceremony as he spoke to them, often angrily it seemed, saying that the Black Robes' way was the only way, that their god was the only god.

Henry never asked his father why he went to the Black Robe church, but he understood. He was amused at One Bull's patience and tolerance toward the Black Robe men. His demeanor was like that which an elder displayed to an unruly child. But he did ask his father why he took food to the wife and daughter of Fork Tail every week, as well as taking the time to gather and haul firewood for them.

"Because it is our way to take care of those among us who have need. We were taught to see to the widows and orphans," One Bull said with quiet conviction.

For Henry, that reply was more meaningful than anything the Black Robes had to say.

The years went by. Henry began courting the daughter of Fork Tail, much to his parents' surprise and joy. One Bull was sad, however, that his old friend the medicine man was not around to know what was happening. After a year, Henry and Sarah were married. Of course, the ceremony had to be performed by the Black Robes. Then

One Bull helped his son build onto Fork Tail's house, and there Henry started his new life.

The following year, Henry found a new job with the railroad, which was building the iron road south of the reservation. He earned enough money to build a bigger house for his family, and one for his parents as well. Esther had married by then. She and her husband built a log house on her father's land, with One Bull's help.

It was in the Moon of Popping Trees—February, as the whites called it—that One Bull fell ill with a cough. His lungs became heavy, and it was difficult for him to breathe. One day he sent for his son.

Henry was surprised to see how frail his father had become. Strangely, however, there was a strong light in his old eyes. On a cold afternoon, One Bull asked his son to walk with him. He took Henry to the dead stump and took out the bag with the black pipe, its stem, and the tobacco. The young man was surprised. He never knew his father had a pipe. They walked to the clearing in the thicket on the hill. There, as Henry watched, his father loaded his pipe with tobacco.

Before he offered his prayers, he grabbed his son's hand and held it. His grip was still strong, though he had to cough frequently. Looking into his son's eyes, he said, "The world would be sad without us who are Lakota. There must always be Lakota in the world."

When he finished praying, One Bull gave the pipe and its accouterments to Henry. Then he made a simple, heartfelt request of his son.

One Bull died on the fourteenth day of the Moon of Popping Trees. As his family sat with him the night before, Henry told him that a grandchild was on the way. He would never forget his father's smile.

Henry and his brother-in-law dug a grave in the clearing in the thicket on the hill. It was hard work because the ground was frozen. As he had requested, Alice and Esther wrapped One Bull in an old elk robe, a robe his mother had given to him. Word of his death had been sent to only a few friends and relatives, who came to bury One Bull. A man sang an honoring song for the old warrior, and afterward they feasted in his honor.

Several days later, one of the Black Robes from the mission went to Henry's house. News of One Bull's passing had finally reached them. The priest was angry that they had not been part of the burial ceremony. Though he demanded to know where One Bull had been buried, Henry declined to tell him. That was also his father's request. Henry smiled patiently at the irritated Black Robe, the way one does to an unruly child.

The Black Robes would never know where One Bull was buried. Nor would they know that a pipe had been passed to another generation.

In Henry's house was a narrow wooden shelf. It was attached to the wall in the front room. On it were several knives made of shiny, glasslike stone with ash-wood handles. Behind the shelf, out of sight in a slot carved into the log wall, was a pipe.

One Bull had found a way to win.

Held to the Fire

Nearly thirty years ago, I listened to radio commentary on the upcoming class B state high school boys basketball tournament in

South Dakota. Two of eight teams were facing off in the opening game, and both had very similar win-loss records. One commentator picked the more flamboyant of the two teams, the one that had won by margins of ten to twenty points per game, to win the game. The other commentator, however, picked the other team, which had won its games by two- to three-point margins. His rationale was that this team was familiar with the pressure of intense competition and had often battled back to win in very close games, while the other team had not. Not only did the second commentator's pick win the opening game by overcoming a ten-point margin, but it also went on to win the tournament.

The flamboyant team had not learned mental toughness. No doubt they had all the athletic ability and had learned all the fundamental drills and plays. However, they had not been tested mentally by the stress of close games, where the outcome was often in doubt until the final buzzer. Their opponent in that first game may not have measured up athletically, but that team had plenty of experience in overcoming odds stacked against them. The deciding factor was their mental strength.

Life, however, is not a basketball game. There are all kinds of situations that can make grown men cry, such as a Korean battlefield and a North Korean prisoner-of-war camp. These were the proving grounds for Tibor Rubin, a Hungarian Jew and immigrant serving in the U.S. Army.

The young soldier was ordered by his company commander to cover his company's redeployment off a hill, alone. Armed with only his rifle and a supply of hand grenades, Rubin waited for the enemy to attack his hill. When they did, he fought ferociously, moving from one position to another, firing and throwing grenades and making the enemy think the hill was defended by an entire company. For twenty-four hours, the young soldier kept the enemy from overrunning the hill, successfully protecting his company's withdrawal. Out of ammunition, he finally rejoined his comrades, who were surprised to see him alive.

Some months later, Rubin faced imprisonment for the second time in his life. After his regiment was overrun by the Chinese, he was taken prisoner with several other surviving soldiers and moved to a North Korean prisoner-of-war camp. To put it mildly, the American soldiers were mistreated, underfed, and received no medical treatment. The young Hungarian immigrant drew on his experience in a Nazi concentration camp during World War II to encourage his fellow prisoners. He taught them to survive on the most minimal supplies of food, some of which he stole—at the risk of his life—from the prison kitchen. Because Rubin had been held to the fire in a similar situation, he knew it was possible to survive starvation, sickness, cold, and beatings. Drawing on that unimaginable experience, he worked hard at keeping his fellow prisoners from falling into despair. Eventually, the American prisoners were released in a prisoner exchange.

A few years later, Tibor Rubin became an American citizen. Several more years were to pass, however, before he was awarded the Medal of Honor for his heroism on the battlefield. Waiting for that medal because his paperwork had been "lost" was probably inconsequential compared to what he had been through on the battlefield and in the prison camp.

Most of us do not have to face and experience the kind of hardship Tibor Rubin did in combat and in two prison camps. Most of our daily problems pale in comparison, but the fact that Rubin did not allow horrific situations to defeat him mentally is an example for the rest of us, or should be. Many problems seem insurmountable to us, and we may be convinced that we do not have the knowledge, experience, or ability to overcome them. But as Rubin showed, the first step to solving or overcoming a problem is simply to face it. That step is, more often than not, followed with action.

Facing up to a problem and taking action does not guarantee success. Thomas Edison engaged in hundreds of failed attempts to make a lightbulb before he succeeded. But when he talked about his failures, he said he had simply found hundreds of ways not to make a lightbulb. As Edison indicates, facing a tough situation is, in and of itself, perhaps the most important part of the process. Once we have done so, no matter the outcome, we have learned not to quit. And knowing that we should not give up is powerful knowledge to have.

Adversity does come into our lives in many forms, be they problems, obstacles, or challenges that each of us contend with over the course of our personal or professional lives. We have probably learned that there are two basic ways to deal with these things; hope that they will eventually go away, or face them. However we choose to deal with such things, we should know and understand that they are opportunities to gain emotional and mental toughness.

Adversity can range from mild and monotonous to gut-wrenching, heartbreaking, and life threatening. Our initial reaction can range from detachment to feeling fear and intimidation—all of which are understandable. Early on, rather than later, should come the conscious decision to deal with the situation. Facing anything can and will strengthen us, giving us an experience and a character attribute that we can always draw on. We can be like the green ash bow that my grandfather held over the heat of the bed of coals. The heat dried and cured it and made it strong.

Over the years, I have thought of that particular bow. Sadly, it was lost in one of the several moves we made over time. But how it came to be and how it performed the way it did remain significant and enduring lessons for me. Undeniably, my grandfather's knowledge and skill were significant factors, because without them, the stave would not have been transformed into that bow. But its strength came from being held to the fire.

I can recall the exact moment I equated that stave in the fire with life. It was as a young adult, after I had come through an extremely difficult period. If there is one certainty in life, it is this: life can hold us to the fire at any time and in any way, whether we are ready or not. The other certainty is that the last time we were held to the fire will not be the last time.

Any experienced bow maker knows that heat is the most effective catalyst. In our everyday lives, adversity is the catalyst that can, and does, build strength. Every morning, all of us face another day. Some of us face the prospect of mundane routine, whether it is commuting to work or attending to the various needs and comfort of our families. Or perhaps it is dealing with heartbreak or grief or an enormously difficult decision. No one is exempt from difficulty, from having to overcome obstacles of some sort.

Too many times there seems to be no immediate answer or solution in sight, no end to the problems that burden us day in and day out. During those times, we do not stop to think that the situation is teaching us to be strong or that we are developing character. But if there is anything to be gained from problems and difficulty—other than solving and surviving them—it is strength and character. The story of Tibor Rubin teaches us that lesson, and so does the story of Henry One Bull.

Luckily, there are also other ways to learn it. My grandparents realized that, as a five-year-old, I was afraid of the dark. Neither of them scolded or even came close to criticizing me for it. In fact, they said nothing at all. As it happened, one of my chores was to keep the woodbins full. One bin was inside the enclosed porch, and the other was next to the cook stove. In the summer, keeping them full was not as critical, but my grandmother still needed wood for cooking.

My grandfather split wood and piled it neatly about thirty yards from the house. Often one of my grandparents would point to the woodbin and ask me to bring in at least one arm-load of wood. For me, that was about four or five pieces. The reminders came usually after dark, which meant I would need to walk to the outside woodpile and back in the dark. I took some comfort in knowing that our dogs were out there, and they would accompany me.

In addition, my grandfather would sometimes pen the horses near the house, especially if we were driving anywhere in the wagon the next day, and sometimes he would ask me to make sure the gate was tied shut and the horses still inside.

Those treks to the horse pen and woodpile, from the time I exited the house to the time I returned, would take all of four minutes—three if my imagination was especially active, and there seemed to be all manner of scary creatures in the dark.

Some evenings, however, my grandfather asked me to accompany him outside, and he would walk around the horse pen, to the root cellar, or one direction or another from the house. There was no reason I could ever figure out for those little nocturnal jaunts. Sometimes he would simply stand and look at the night sky or listen to the various night sounds around us. There was nothing to be afraid of as long as he was there.

It took me a while to figure out that there were things out there in the dark, but nothing that was not there in the daylight, and not the things my imagination was trying to convince me were there. In time, I got over my fear of the dark. Now, just about every time I see the sun go down, I remember how cleverly, quietly, and lovingly my grandparents taught me how to be strong.

Emotional, mental, and spiritual strength is the first line of defense against hardship and difficulty. It is an attribute that we cannot buy or barter to attain. And funny enough, in order to face hardship with strength, we have to first learn to be strong by experiencing hardship. Learning to be strong is rather like receiving a vaccination; we are inoculated with the very disease we need to prevent. We are certainly immersed in that learning process from the moment we are born. Every day is an opportunity, to one extent or another, to learn how to be strong by living life.

Not everyone's life circumstance is the same. While there are general demographic categories we fit into, individual circumstances are different; there are billions of stories out there. We do not all live in a city or in a rural area. Our religious beliefs vary; so do our income levels, living conditions, family makeup, education, and so on. But there are two factors (realities, if you will) we all have in common: not a single one of us asked to be born, and none of us knows exactly how our lives will turn out. It is the journey in between that shapes each of us into who and what we are.

My father never imagined he would lose his nineteen-year-old brother, even though both of them were in the army and deployed to combat zones in the Pacific in World War II. Death and injury were definite possibilities, but when possibility became reality, it was a shock.

In early 1945, my father was on Okinawa with an Eighth Army Air Force engineer battalion. After his unit had helped in mop-up operations, they built prisoner-of-war camps for the Japanese soldiers who had surrendered or were captured. My uncle was on the island of Luzon in the Philippines, assigned to a headquarters company in the 44th Infantry Division.

Communication between my father and uncle was sporadic, a few letters here and there. They were kept informed of each other's situations mainly through my grandparents, who were in touch with both of them via letters. My mother also wrote to both of them regularly. However, during wartime, mail from the States often took weeks to reach a combat zone.

On the night of June 12, 1945, my father was on sentry duty at one of the camps he had helped to build. His post was outside the fence and between two light posts. In between the lights were the gate and a gravel road coming out of the gate. Armed with an M1 rifle, he patrolled the area between the two light posts. About halfway into his watch, he heard something or someone walking behind him just after he passed the roadbed. He heard footsteps on the gravel. But when he turned to challenge what he thought was an intruder—possibly an escaped prisoner—there was nothing.

He carefully and thoroughly surveyed the area with his flashlight, but found nothing. When he resumed his patrol, he heard the footsteps again. Though he reacted again, the outcome was the same. No one, other than him, was in the area. I believe he said he reported the possibility of an escaped prisoner to the corporal of the guard, but a head count revealed that all prisoners were present and accounted for in that sector.

The incident bothered him. He had heard his share of ghost stories, and the footsteps on the gravel certainly were something of a ghostly occurrence, or at least an occurrence not easily explained.

Then he received news from the Red Cross that explained the footsteps, as far as my father was concerned. A telegram informed him that his younger brother had been wounded on June 8 and died of his wounds on June 12, the same day my dad had been on sentry duty.

My father told me the story only once. I had to ask my mother when I wanted to hear it again, and she repeated it exactly as he had told it. It was not until years later, as a young adult, that I understood two comments my father had made about that incident. First, he believed the footsteps had been made by the spirit of his brother, who had come to say good-bye. Second, the footsteps (and his brother's visit) had prepared him for the news of his brother's death. Though the news was heartbreaking, it did not take him completely by surprise. He was always grateful to his younger brother for preparing him, for "softening the blow."

One of the lessons that I take away from my father's story of the footsteps on the gravel is that life does teach us to be strong—or it certainly can if we let it. It is not necessary to believe in ghosts; we just need to do what we can every day to get through each day. And somewhere in that succession of days, more often than we realize, will be the incidents, occurrences, and events that are the life lessons.

No Greater Treasure

Sir David Lean (1908–1991), the British director, producer, and screenwriter of epic films such as *Lawrence of Arabia*, *The Bridge on the River Kwai*, *Doctor Zhivago*, and *A Passage to India*, late in his career wanted to pitch a new project to a major studio. He was initially interviewed by a twenty-something gatekeeper, who knew nothing of Lean and his accomplishments.

The first words out of the young man's mouth were, "Tell me what you've done."

To which Lean replied, "You first."

I cannot vouch for the veracity of the story, but it feels true, and I have a feeling anyone over fifty wants it to be true. Whatever the case, it does, unfortunately, speak to a truism. We live in a youth-oriented world that has no place for white hair and a slower pace. It is a sad consequence of the demise of the village, the loss of that traditional structure of many cultures wherein the knowledge and experience of old people rested at the top. Consequently, many children no longer have the consistent influence of grandparents through their formative years.

Most of the people who populated my childhood were old. They were contemporaries, friends, and relatives of all of my grandparents. My formative years were spent with my grandparents, mostly with my maternal grandparents, Albert and Annie Two Hawk. As a matter of fact, except for two of the years from middle school to high school, they were always nearby and, for those two years, not more than 150 miles away. The opportunities to see and spend time with my paternal grandparents were frequent, and they were never more than 150 miles away. All of them lived into their eighties and were part of my life well past my childhood and into my midthirties.

As a child, I did not regard my grandparents as old. Chronological age was not part of my awareness. The primary perception I had of all of them was that they knew everything and could do anything. Moreover, all of them had a sense of humor and liked to tease. My grandfather Albert told me that his first job was working in a place where macaroni was made. He said he drilled the holes and then bent the macaroni.

I was fortunate (to say the least) to have been a child in a time and in a place where grandparents and elders in general were an integral part of the community—obviously much more than they are now. Nothing stood in the way of the natural bond that children and elders have with each other. Any kind of social gathering did not seem normal unless there were elders there. At all such occasions, at least one elder was asked to talk, to impart words of wisdom regarding the occasion. But the occasions at which elders always spoke were wakes and memorial feasts for someone who had died. Those were the times when their wisdom and insight were especially needed. I cannot remember any instance when an elder was not the epitome of compassion, sensitivity, grace, and wisdom. They always had a way to comfort and uplift, and thereby strengthen, with their words.

In my childhood, my connection and interaction with my grandparents and other elders were not diluted or affected by outside influences, such as telephones and e-mails. All interaction was face-to-face: me listening or watching them work and them telling stories, teaching me how to do something, or explaining something. Furthermore, no negative attitudes got in the way, especially from me. I had the feeling that all elders deserved my respect and good behavior. How and when I learned that is not a clear memory, but it was part of me nonetheless. All of these factors strengthened and empowered my relationship with them.

As far as I can tell, my generation was likely and sadly at the end of the time when elders had a significant role in the life of the village. Today, there are still Lakota grandmas and grandpas, but recent Lakota generations have been influenced by the mainstream society's youth-oriented attitude. Hence, that natural bond between elders and children has been diminished. But in the old days, the wisdom of the elders was the guiding influence for family and community. That wisdom was the way villages governed themselves.

The hierarchy of leadership was simple. From top to bottom it was:

wicahcala omniciye
Gathering of Old Men, or village council

wapiya wicasa
medicine men

wicasa itancan na zuya itancan
civilian leaders and military leaders

zuya wica na zuya wicasa omniciyapi
warriors and warrior societies

oyate kin
the people, or general population

Except for certain instances, such as a village breaking camp and moving, this system functioned without authority that could be enforced. In fact, the word *authority* did not exist in the pre-reservation Lakota language, nor did the concept. (Since then, non-Lakota linguists and lexicographers have used words and phrases to represent the word *authority*, since they did not accept the fact that it did not exist in the language.)

Everyone had a voice in two ways whenever the Gathering of Old Men met. First, the old men did not speak for themselves; they spoke for the people. As a matter of fact, another informal title given to each of the old men individually was *woglake wicasa*, or "the man who speaks." And the expectation and implication was that he spoke *for* the people. The second way that everyone had a voice was that individuals were often invited in to speak to the gathering.

The old men themselves would talk about an issue or a problem at length, sometimes for days on end. When they had come to a conclusion, they announced it to the people in the form of advice, not as a directive or an order. But given that any gathering of elders collectively represented hundreds of years of experience and was an astounding repository of combined knowledge, the people listened carefully and, more often than not, did what the old men advised.

The wisdom of elders was the guiding influence in family and community life for the Lakota people for untold generations. That influence ended when the U.S. Congress enacted the Indian Reorganization Act (IRA) of 1934. One of the changes the IRA brought to Indian country was the formulation of tribal governments patterned after the U.S. government, with a legislative, executive, and judicial branch. The beginning of the end was in 1877. The various Lakota bands were placed on separate reservations, all of them west of the Missouri River, in what was still then Dakota Territory. It may be somewhat accurate to say or assume that the various bands had no form of government, traditional or otherwise. But there was no lack of leadership. Men like Spotted Tail of the Sicangu Lakota and Sitting Bull of the Hunkpapa Lakota (once he had returned from Canada) and others were still regarded as leaders by their peoples. But the cohesive and powerful influence of pre-reservation village councils was essentially gone.

The IRA was the last nail in the coffin because of one simple condition: the minimum age for election to the tribal legislature was set at twenty-five. The tribes were given constitutions modeled after the United States constitution—condensed versions, as it were. Eligibility qualifications were established to determine who could stand for election to the tribal legislature, which were called councils. One of these requirements was a minimum age, which was twenty-five.

The issue of age was not an immediate factor because people, by and large, knew and understood the role of elders. They still saw them as the ultimate source of wisdom. So for the most part, older men were elected to the first councils. Though those first councils were largely powerless and mostly ceremonial in nature, people still saw the necessity of electing men who "had been there and done that," so to speak—men who had lived life.

But after a generation or so, younger men began to win election to the tribal council. The commitment of those young men is not the issue, nor is their dedication to working for the welfare of the people, at least in most cases. But the life experiences of people in their twenties and thirties do not compare to those of someone who is sixty or older.

If we fast-forward to today's tribal councils, it is a safe assumption that most of their members are between the ages of twenty-five and forty. Compare that to the pre-reservation days, when the basic requirement to sit in the Gathering of Old

Men was to have survived into old age. To survive into old age meant a lifetime of experience and knowledge that was the basis for wisdom.

If there is any fundamental weakness with today's tribal councils, it is that single factor: youth. True, there are tribal council members who may have education and experience, but anyone below the age of sixty does not have the requisite life experiences to fully bring that education and experience to bear. Throw in factional politics, and we have tribal councils full of politicians, but no real leaders.

The same applies to tribal chairmen, chairwomen, presidents, and governors. Youth is their greatest liability. Tribal constitutions, and for that matter, the U.S. and state constitutions, should be amended to raise the minimum age for elected officeholders across the board to sixty—no ifs, ands, or buts.

The end of the free-roaming, nomadic lifestyle more or less brought wholesale change to the Lakota culture, change that impacted everyone and every aspect of life. It was hard on everyone but arguably hardest on men between their late teens and midforties. They were the hunters and warriors in the most physically active stage of their lives. Part of change, however, required that hunters and warriors give up their guns and horses. It was no longer necessary for them to hunt because the government now provided food. There was no more fighting, because the Lakota had surrendered to white authority. In essence, there was no longer any use for the hunter/warrior.

If not for two groups, Lakota culture probably would not have survived the period between 1870 and 1940. Those two groups were the women and the elders.

Women simply kept doing what they had done for countless generations—being nurturers and the backbones of families. To put it bluntly, they kept their families together even as their husbands and sons were floundering, trying to find a place and a purpose in the new life under white authority. It was during this time that alcoholism gained a foothold, adding another burden for families to deal with.

The elders, meanwhile, were also a source of strength. They reminded everyone that the best way to endure and survive the new order was for Lakota people to remember who they were, that living like the white people did not mean being like the white people.

The circumstances required the Lakota to be strong. No one can convince me otherwise: were it not for women and elders rising to the challenge when their people were the most vulnerable, Lakota culture might have been a total loss; assimilation might have won.

There were losses, however, and perhaps one of the most profound is the loss of our Lakota regard for elders. There has been a disconnect in that regard, primarily because we have bought into the mainstream society's attitude toward elders. Now it is not unusual for us, like most people, to relegate our elders to nursing homes, which is a far cry from the revered place the elderly traditionally had in the Lakota family and community.

In the nomadic era, the lodges of the elderly were not pitched in the "elder section." There was no such place. Old people usually lived next door to their children. Widows and widowers often lived with their children, making a three-generation household.

Interestingly enough, nursing homes (or rest homes or assisted living facilities) are a relatively recent phenomenon. Generally speaking, that approach to elder care began in the nineteenth century, with church groups establishing special homes for elderly people, usually for a particular ethnic or religious background. During the early twentieth century, there was no government assistance, so the impoverished (or disabled) elderly were relegated to institutions called almshouses. Unfortunately, conditions in such places were bad, and the care provided was often questionable. By and large, separate care facilities were not always the best places for the old and the infirm until laws were passed to standardize care and establish guidelines. Even into the mid-1980s, states and the federal government were still wrestling with issues of standardized care and funding for nursing homes.

Recent statistics indicate that 20 percent of the American population is fourteen years and under, 67 percent is between the ages of fifteen and sixty-four, and nearly 13 percent is sixty-five or older. In approximate numbers, the last category comprises 39 million people.

Those 39 million people have a combined *2 billion, 535 million* years of life experience. There is no greater treasure or resource.

It would be safe to assume that there are several reasons for what I call the "elderly disconnect" in American society (and Western society in general). It is not, however, the elderly disconnecting themselves from the younger generations. It is most definitely the other way around. One of the reasons is that we are a mobile society; we move frequently owing to jobs and careers. Most people stay at one job for an average of four years and then change. Over a lifetime, people have seven to ten different jobs. Upward or lateral mobility in a job or career translates into geographic movement. Families become scattered and disconnected, some to a greater extent than others. In doing so, they separate themselves from the influence of grandparents.

One statistic that recently floated across the public airwaves suggests that married couples make up only 48 percent of American households. If that is accurate, it would mean that what we perceived to be the traditional relationship between children and grandparents is also probably not what it once was. The current high rate of divorce and the formulation of blended, or "step," families also adversely impacts that relationship. Much of what we once considered traditional in family life has changed. There are no longer clearly defined roles. But these changes should not completely sever the emotional ties between children and grandparents. There are other ways to connect.

Elders are still viable sources of wisdom, and though the times of listening to stories on a long winter night in their houses are long gone for most of us, technology provides a way to stay connected. My daughters will respond immediately to text messages, and staying connected to elders that way is better than not being connected. My generation needs to learn how to use a smart phone and to keep up with aspects of technology we never dreamed would exist; if that is what it takes to stay connected to children and grandchildren, so be it. The love of grandma and grandpa carried in a voice mail, an e-mail, or a text message is still genuine, even if it is not accompanied by hugs. Likewise, the wisdom of elders transported across cyberspace is just as valuable.

Though I do miss the hugs. Being from the generation I am, I prefer the eye-to-eye, heart-to-heart connection. I shudder to think that we are part of a time when there is less and less of that.

One of my favorite stories comes out of the boarding-school era on the Rosebud Reservation. A friend of mine told about her mother's experience at the reservation's only parochial boarding school when her mother was seven years old. She and a friend were severely punished after they were caught speaking Lakota, which was against school (and government) policy. During the summer break, the girl told her grandmother about the incident.

The grandmother sympathized with her granddaughter and then gave her one piece of advice. She told her, "Next time, whisper."

Wisdom is the basis for strength in any society, culture, or nation. And the source of wisdom is in our elders. It is the epitome of stupidity and arrogance to ignore that reality.

5

Resiliency

A Quiet Woman

She lived along the river west of the highway. Her little
log house was the first in what became known as Lower
Bent Creek Village. In fact, it was there before the freight
wagon road through the reservation became a gravel road
and then an official highway. She worked side by side with
her husband to build that house. He died a couple of years
after it was finished. Later she added on to it by herself
without asking anyone for help. That was her way, never
asking anyone for help.

Even people who were not related to her called her
Grandma Red Leaf. Though it was more or less known
that her first name was Molly, she disdained that name
because it had been given to her by a white man at
the agency. She and her sister had gone to sign papers
for the land they had inherited when their father died.
When she was a girl and before the whites were in
control, her name was Flying High. Her mother gave
her that name because she liked to watch the geese fly
overhead. Red Leaf had been her husband's name. She
never understood how the whites used names, no matter

how many times her granddaughter tried to explain it to her.

As near as her granddaughter could figure it, Grandma Red Leaf had been born in 1870. She was a widow for twenty years before she died in 1951, not long after her second son was killed in Korea. (He had been a soldier in the army and had fought in World War II as well.) Even though she had gone blind four years before she died, she had continued living alone. Her independence astounded everyone. She could start a fire in her cookstove and had laid out a path to the river for herself in order to haul water.

My grandparents and I lived several miles farther west, and we stopped at Grandma Red Leaf's house each time we went to town, which was at least once a month from late spring to late fall. She was always happy to see us. Often we would spend the night, and my grandmother would cook a big pot of soup. The leftovers would last Grandma Red Leaf for days and days. In the fall, my grandfather and other men in the community would lay in wood for her, enough to last her through the winter. Years later, I realized that the families who lived in Lower Bent Creek, though their houses were miles apart, were still a village. That is why everyone took care of Grandma Red Leaf. My grandparents, among others, had asked her to come and live with us. She could not leave her memories, she would always say—the memories of her family connected to her place.

Two things about that old woman I will never forget. She had snow white hair since the first time I remember seeing her, likely when I was four. Always she wore two braids, but what fascinated me was that sometimes she braided thin strips of red wool into her hair. Then there were her hands. Every time we stopped to visit, she insisted on touching my face. Her hands were gnarled and very strong. I asked my grandmother about the occasional strips of red cloth in Grandma Red Leaf's braids. She told me I should ask Grandma Red Leaf about those, but she did make a statement about the old woman's hands.

"She worked hard all her life," my grandmother said. "She hauled wood, chopped wood, sewed, cooked, and butchered animals. There was nothing she could not do. She was especially good at trimming horses' hooves. But that is not the only reason her hands are strong. They are strong because her spirit is strong. Grandma Red Leaf has had a very hard life."

If that was the case, I could never tell. Perhaps it was because I was far too young to see the kinds of things older people did, and they certainly knew a lot more than I did about the past.

On one visit, I finally got the nerve to ask Grandma Red Leaf about the strips of red wool. It was a summer's day, and we were sitting in the shade of a small oak tree.

"Come here, Grandson," she said. "Bring us coffee, and I will tell you."

Her voice was always soft and a little raspy. I brought the coffee, one for her and one for me, and put the cups on a sawn stump of log. She always sat to the left side of one, on an old chair someone had given her.

"When I was a little girl, six or seven, I lived with my grandmother, like you do," she began. It was where the whites took us before they brought us up here. But one summer, we left that place and went north, to join Crazy Horse and his people. You have heard of Crazy Horse?"

By then I had heard a few stories of Crazy Horse.

"He was in the Powder River country with his people because he did not like the whites. He wanted nothing

to do with them. In the winter, we were told that he and
Sitting Bull would bring the people together. That is why
we went north. We joined them when they were at Ash
Creek. I have never seen so many people together at one
time—too many to count. There were more horses than
people, too.

"There was a Sun Dance, and then we moved west to
a big open valley, along a river called Greasy Grass. We
pitched our lodge in the northern part of the village.
My mother and father and my grandmother and I lived
together in a small lodge. It was made of buffalo hide, thin
and patched, but it was our home.

"The morning after we moved there, I went to pick
berries with my mother and grandmother. From where
we were, we could see the horses. They filled the whole
valley to the west. Back at our lodge, my mother started
pounding the berries, and my grandmother and I went to
the river. We were looking for mint, so we could have tea.
We were on our way back when the guns started shooting.
Our men started yelling; women were calling for their
children. Everyone was running around.

"At first we did not know who was attacking us; then
someone said it was the Long Knives. Back at our lodge,
my mother said my father had gone with the other men
to fight the Long Knives. Then she left to help someone
find their children.

"The Long Knives were coming from the south,
someone said. We could hear the firing get closer and
closer, but we stayed in our lodge. Then the sounds of the
guns grew faint. After a while, many of the men came
back through the village, and then the guns started firing
to the east across the river. We were told there were many
Long Knives, but they were stopped before they charged

into the village. Now they were east across the river and being chased to the north.

"The whole time, people were running around. Men came back through the village again. We heard that some of the wounded men were being helped at the south end. My grandmother was worried about my father. We did not know where he was. My grandmother suddenly took me by the hand and took me east toward the river.

"A group of men and boys told us that the fighting was going north now, away from us. We could hear the guns still firing, but we kept going and waded across the river. After that, we circled around some low hills and went up to a flat. All the time, we heard the guns firing. At the end of the flat, we saw our men above us on a ridge to the east. They were riding after the Long Knives, chasing them north. Some were shooting with guns, some with bows and arrows.

"We stopped there. All we could do was watch. Then my grandmother started singing. She sang Strong Heart songs to encourage our men. A few of our men came up from the river or rode close to us. They heard my grandmother singing. She kept singing.

"After awhile, it was quiet. No more guns shooting. We looked and looked, but we could not see my father anywhere. A man came—a Cheyenne, a Dog Soldier—and then one of our Crazy Dog men. They both got off their horses and gave my grandmother their fighting sashes, the long red sashes they wore. These were very brave fighting men, those Dog Soldiers and Crazy Dogs. Sometimes they pegged themselves to one spot to fight and fought there until they were killed or they won. They each thanked my grandmother for singing for them.

"We went back to the village. My mother was there, and later my father came back. The next day there was more fighting back to the south. Some Long Knives were surrounded on a hill. Then the whole village broke camp, and we moved away to the south.

"My grandmother kept those sashes with her things. One day she cut off some strips and gave them to me. Sometimes when I miss her, I braid them into my hair."

My grandfather had talked about that battle, so I did know something about it. The Greasy Grass Fight, our people called it. Others called it the Battle of the Little Bighorn. The last time I saw those red wool sashes was when Grandma Red Leaf died. My grandmother and a lot of other women prepared her for burial, and she was put into a wood casket someone had brought from the agency. The red strips were braided into her hair.

When she had finished her story, that day in the shade of the oak tree, Grandma Red Leaf sang a Strong Heart song—one of the songs her grandmother had sung that day long ago. To this day, every time I hear a warriors' honoring song, I think of her.

During her wake, people came from all around, even a few whites. Old people stood and talked about Grandma Red Leaf. Never could I have imagined what I heard.

Her father had fought at the Battle of the Little Bighorn and had not suffered so much as a scratch. In December of 1890, he had gone looking for a relative who had been part of the Ghost Dances in the Stronghold, a hiding place in the Badlands. Somehow he had been caught up in the capture of Big Foot's band and was at Wounded Knee Creek with them. He had been one of the nearly three hundred men, women, and children killed when the Long Knives opened fire on December 29.

Grandma Red Leaf's mother and grandmother had both sickened and died of influenza, her grandmother in

1896 and her mother in 1919. She had married in 1900 and had three children. Two of them died, one as an infant, and her second son was killed in Korea. Her husband had died in 1940.

But not only did the old ones talk about the tragedies in Grandma Red Leaf's life—some of them weeping as they did—they also talked about the kind of person she was. To all of them, she was the epitome of strength and grace. She never blamed anyone or anything for all the hardships she had faced and endured, they said. Instead, she was always grateful for all the good things that happened, though it seemed to me there was more bad than good.

My grandparents talked about Grandma Red Leaf often, though they never called her by her name after she died. They referred to her as the Blind One or the Blind Old Woman. Anytime they spoke of her, it was with obvious respect and the deepest affection. In one of those conversations, my grandfather likened the Blind Old Woman to a bow.

"A bow is drawn many, many times to send its arrows," he said. "And each time, it returns to what it was, ready to send the next arrow. No matter what happened to that Blind Old Woman, she was always the same as she was before—a strong and quiet woman."

I have lost count of how many times I have thought about Grandma Red Leaf over the years. Each time, I remember my grandfather's metaphor. Several times I tried to come up with an English word to describe the essence of that old woman as my grandparents saw her. Finally, many years ago I did.

That word is *resiliency*.

To Go On

An amazing characteristic of a primitive Lakota bow is its resiliency. There are at least three reasons for that: one is the wood the bow maker selected, the second is the simple and effective design of the bow, and the third is the skill of the craftsman.

People can become resilient as well, because we are taught values and develop characteristics that give us that potential. The "bow maker" includes several factors or forces, the most important of which is our upbringing. As most sociologists and psychologists agree, much of what we will be is formed in the first few years of life. After that, everything that we learn and experience further shapes us, just as the bow maker shapes the bow's limbs to withstand the stress of being drawn back. During its life, that bow is drawn thousands and thousands of times; it is stressed toward its breaking point each time. During our lives, we will be tested just as the bow is—we will be stressed, as it were—by the trials and tribulations we face.

Life is tough. That is one of the few realities we should be taught the moment we reach the age of discretion. Life is not only tough, but it is also often convoluted. Life is also good, but good does not mean the complete absence of problems, disappointment, heartbreak, grief, and the other things that make life tough. Handling the good times, meaning the periods when the tough situations are absent, however long or brief they are, is not difficult. Handling the tough times is. Ironically, knowing that tough times are part of life goes a long way to helping us get through them.

There are no magic wands that can make bad things go away. But I think there is something that can help us make it through the bad times. All four of my immediate grandparents had one ability or characteristic, one part of their character, that was as important as any other: resiliency.

My paternal grandfather, the Reverend Charles J. Marshall, died in late December of 1974. For forty years, he was an ordained Episcopalian deacon, as his father, Joseph, had been. Grandpa Charles was a tall, distinguished-looking man with an imposing presence, a baritone voice, silvery white hair, and startling blue eyes. The last feature was a consequence of his French blood. (As a soldier in World War I, he was shipped to France and fought in his father's homeland.)

I have many enduring memories of Grandpa Charles. He was an avid fisherman and very athletic, still playing baseball at the age of fifty-five, white hair and all. My father, Joseph II, inherited that baseball prowess. Unfortunately, I did not. But I will be happy if I have one grain of my grandfather's resiliency.

In 1972, at age eighty-five, he suffered a stroke, which affected his movement and slurred his speech somewhat. For a man who led a physically active life and had been a powerful orator, this had to have been a devastating blow. But he still stood straight, though he walked with a bit of a shuffle and had to choose his words carefully. If he complained, I never heard about it. It was after that stroke that I saw just how dignified he was. He simply did not let a very difficult circumstance diminish his will and spirit. Only another and more serious stroke took him down.

He and my grandmother Blanche had a long life together. She outlived him by ten years. Together they lived through their share of difficulty. The first loss was their first son, who died at the age of three. (My grandmother was a widow and also had a son, my uncle Narcisse Brave, with her first husband.) They lost their third son in June of 1945, my father's younger brother, Melvin, who was killed in one of the last major infantry operations in the Pacific in World War II. He was nineteen.

I lived with my paternal grandparents for the first two years of school. While there, I remember seeing a wooden plaque on the wall near the table my grandfather used as his desk. Not until years later, after they had moved back to the Rosebud Reservation, did I take a closer look at it. It was the Gold Star plaque, commemorating my uncle Melvin's "full measure of devotion." On it was a facsimile of President Harry S. Truman's signature.

On several occasions, both my grandparents told me about my uncle. They spoke softly, never calling him by name, referring to him as "your uncle who was killed." At that point, it was nearly ten years since they had lost him. They still grieved. I could hear their grief in their voices and see it on their faces. They did not talk about him being killed; they told me about his childhood and about his escapades with my dad. Though they chose to remember his brief life with stories of boyish things and good times, sometimes even laughing, my grandmother would invariably dab at her tears with a handkerchief. My grandfather always concluded comments about his youngest son with, "He was a good boy."

I never sensed any amount of bitterness from either of them. They were simply happy to have had him in their lives. They said similar things about their first son, Irvin, as well.

I cannot imagine how it feels to lose a child. One of my sisters and a first cousin each have. Children's deaths are a sad fact of life, but those who suffered this kind of heartrending loss somehow endure it the best way they could. That, to me, is resiliency.

Life teaches us to be resilient. We enroll in Resiliency 101 the moment we are born, because life is tough. Sometimes life hands us a circumstance in which there are two choices: handle it or run. Another of my cousins and her husband found themselves in just that kind of a tough predicament. Their only son contracted spinal meningitis. It reduced him to a homebound invalid, taking both his legs. Not only did they have to design their home to accommodate a totally dependent son, but they also had to adapt their lives to meet his every need. Only occasionally do they leave his care in the hands of third-party caretakers. I am sure from time to time they have asked why life chose to give them such a burden. But I marvel at their devotion to their son. For me, they are the most profound examples of parental love and commitment. They are showing anyone who is paying attention how to be resilient.

It often is not necessary to look beyond family to see examples of character. My aunts, my father's five sisters—Adelia Marshall White, Opal Marshall Stars, Margaret Marshall Krieger, LaVera Marshall Bull Bear, and Charlotte Marshall Weston—are such examples. They range in age from just over seventy to nearly ninety. Three of them are widows, one for thirty years. One of them, at age eighty-four, was a passenger in a car crash that killed her son-in-law. She suffered serious injuries and endured months of physical therapy just to walk again. Two of her sisters have faced (or are facing) serious health issues. Nevertheless, they are all the epitome of grace.

The year 2011 marks ten years that my mother, Hazel Two Hawk Marshall, has been a widow, as she reached her eighty-third birthday. She lives in the same house she shared with my father, where most of her children grew up. She has seen some hard times in the past ten years, in the last six months of 2010 especially. Yet, like her sisters-in-law, she lives life one day at a time, meets every difficulty with quiet grace, and savors the good times.

My mother and my aunts have one thing in common, other than being family: all of them have a deep and abiding faith in their God, the kind that can move mountains. It is empowering to see them together. Those moments are special because their strength of spirit and resiliency are almost palpable, like a tangible mist that one wants to bathe in to absorb as much as possible.

My aunts and my mother were not born resilient. Life taught them resiliency; it forged them into strong women. I am certain that none of them wanted to face the kinds of heartbreak, loss, and innumerable obstacles they experienced and endured. Furthermore, they did not overcome every difficult situation; they did not win every battle. But without a doubt, they faced every situation and fought back, drawing on the values they learned and the character they had developed. All of them are cut from the same cloth as Grandma Red Leaf.

Anytime I think about resiliency, the focus invariably goes to my grandparents. Each of them, except for my maternal grandmother, was born before 1900, the year she was born. Their generation was the swing or pivotal one relative to an entire group of people adjusting from one kind of lifestyle to an entirely different one. Their parents were born in the 1860s or a little later, and they had firsthand knowledge of the pre-reservation era. (In late 1877, the Lakota bands were relocated to what is now western South Dakota, onto separate reservations.)

On the paternal side of my ancestry, there is significant French influence. Both my paternal grandparents had parents who were at least second-generation French. My paternal grandmother's maiden name is Roubideaux. The spelling of my paternal great-grandfather's French surname was likely anglicized to Marshall, probably from Marichale or Mareschault (or some other spelling). He married an Oglala Lakota woman, as did his brother.

My maternal grandparents were Sicangu Lakota. Their parents and grandparents had names like Zintka Cika (Little Bird), Wanbli Ho Waste (Good Voice Eagle), Pejuta To Win (Blue Medicine Woman or Woman with the Blue Medicine), and Situpi Ska (White Tail Feathers). But somehow the name McLean shows up in my maternal grandmother's family tree as well. Molly McLean was my maternal great-grandmother, and she married Good Voice Eagle, a traditional healer or medicine man. He died at the age of forty-nine, and eventually Grandma Molly married again, to a man named Charles Lodgeskin.

For anyone of us, no matter who we are, to know our family history is to know at least a part of the history of a given group of people, of a particular period in time or of a particular region. If we are fortunate to know the kind of people our ancestors were, then we will have an insight into their contemporaries, because the character and makeup of our ancestors is a reflection of the community or group they are part of.

To say that the period between 1890 and 1940 was strange and stressful for the Lakota people, as they tried to adjust to a restricted and controlled lifestyle on the reservations, would be the understatement of a lifetime. My grandparents and great-grandparents were in the thick of it, and the fact that their generations emerged with their individual sense of identity intact, as well as retaining their culture, is nothing short of a miracle. They were able to do it, individually and collectively, because they were tough and resilient.

As I have said elsewhere in this book, my great-grandparents' generation was completing the hard turn, so to speak, that their parents had started—that is, from the nomadic life of the prairies to the sedentary life of the reservation. They were expected to give up one culture and assimilate to another, as if they were taking off an old pair of shoes and putting on new ones. But the change they had to make was not that easy, not even close.

My maternal grandfather was born two years before the 1890 Wounded Knee massacre. Though his parents were not there (his biological father had died by then), they knew about it because that news traveled fast. Some of what my grandfather knew about that tragic event he heard from people who had been on the Pine Ridge Reservation in December of 1890. Whenever he talked about the massacre (which was not often), he marveled at the courage and resiliency of the people who had lived through it. The last time I heard him talk about it, he concluded with an honoring song for the people who had been killed, singing it softly and using his cupped hands like a drum. It was the only time I ever saw him cry.

I regarded my grandfather as a pillar of strength. So for him to be awed by the strength of his ancestors was a powerful statement. He felt there was no comparison between him and the people who had gone before. He looked up to them, respecting them, what they stood for and what they had done.

From the stories he told about his mother and father and other people, I could tell that my grandfather regarded strength and resiliency as important attributes. According to him (and other of his contemporaries, including relatives and friends), strength enabled you to get through a difficult and even a horrifying occurrence or time, and resiliency enabled you to go on.

The Best You Have

History is replete with examples of the resiliency of the human race. Unfortunately, most of them usually involve one group of people inflicting extreme hardship on another. The Black Hole of Calcutta, the Bataan Death March, the Siberian death camps, the Long Walk of the Navajo (Diné), and the African slave trade are all examples, as are any cases of false imprisonment, forced prostitution, and human trafficking. Then there is rape, homicide, bullying, kidnapping, and beatings. These are atrocities we do not like to read or hear about. (Though in these times, we hear about them almost as soon as they happen, and the reports often come with graphic images.) These are experiences that are far removed from the everyday lives of many, if not most, people. We are shocked and horrified that humans can be so cruel and cold-blooded.

But human cruelty to other humans is not the only cause of hardship. Sometimes we are the victims of our own bad judgment or just plain bad luck or the everyday burdens that befall us and accumulate.

Sadly, people's inhumanity to others will never go away, nor will life's difficulties and hardships. We humans do have a propensity for arrogance, ignorance, stupidity, and cruelty. But we also have the ability to rise to the occasion, collectively and individually, in the face of inhumanity and hardship.

All of my grandparents, at one time and in so many words, said that when life beats you down with the worst it has, the only way to deal with it is with the best you have. That was their definition of resiliency.

Examples of resiliency can be found elsewhere as well, such as in the 1967 feature film *Cool Hand Luke*. Though the movie is known for the iconic line, "What we got here is a failure to communicate," I like it for another reason. The character of Luke, played by Paul Newman, tries to find acceptance among his fellow inmates and challenges the biggest man in the place. In every instance, he is physically overpowered (to put it nicely) by the bigger man, but he never quits. Though he is beaten down time after time, his will to keep trying is not. He gets back on his feet again and again until he is literally too weak to move. In the end, he wins the respect of his antagonist and fellow inmates, not because he wins physically, but because he does not quit.

Like Luke, my grandparents were not quitters. Not only did they define resilience with words, but they also demonstrated it in their lives.

I saw my paternal grandfather maintain his dignity in the face of a debilitating stroke. A short three months later, my maternal grandfather faced the last weeks of his life with equal dignity and strength of spirit.

My grandfather Charles Marshall was an infantry soldier in World War I and fought in France in 1918. He lived through the German mustard-gas attacks and was in some of the worst trench warfare. He went "over the top" several times, meaning he and other soldiers (entire companies, battalions, and regiments) charged up and out of the trenches, often into withering enemy fire. Back home, he worked in the Homestake Gold Mine in the Black Hills at a time when mining was an extremely risky activity. He and my grandmother ran a few head of cattle and planted crops in order to support their growing family. Later, he answered the call to serve in the ministry and patiently plodded his way through a correspondence course in order to qualify. I later learned that he posted one of the highest grades (if not the highest) in that program, ever.

My maternal grandfather, Albert Two Hawk, faced his own challenges. He was about eight years old when his biological father died. It was a struggle for him, his mother, and his sisters just to survive. But he assumed a man's responsibility, making sure his mother and sisters had enough to eat by working odd jobs and hunting. I have somewhat vague memories, as a four-year-old, of him building a log house. He had cut down the trees up to two years before, then hauled them from the river bottom up to the site he and my grandmother had chosen, a distance of three miles. He used big drag horses to pull the logs. Then he peeled the bark off the logs and then cut notches in each one, so they would fit evenly on the corners. Then he had to lift the logs into place. The logs for the lower part of the walls, though by no means easy, were not as hard to lift as those for the upper walls. Logs that had to be lifted four feet and higher were the toughest challenge. For that, he fashioned a tripod brace and used a block-and-tackle pulley and horsepower. All of it was backbreaking work.

Both of my grandmothers outlived their husbands by at least nine years. They shared stories of my grandfathers with me.

These stories were a way for each of them to deal with loneliness and grief. In the end, they too faced death with grace and utterly without fear.

Both of my grandmothers were artisans; creative artistry was among the many skills and abilities they had. They had learned from their mothers and grandmothers the art of beading, which was the logical outgrowth of quillwork. Quilling was a labor-intensive process of harvesting porcupine quills, drying and dyeing them, and then applying them to artifacts and clothing using one of at least seventeen different appliqué methods. Glass beads, traded by Europeans, replaced quills and immediately became popular with the women of many tribes. But beadwork required just as much skill, dedication, and an eye for color and pattern design.

Grandma Blanche Marshall made traditional Lakota moccasins and sewed beads directly onto the leather. The process required piercing holes in the tanned leather, stringing beads onto the thread, sewing down the strings, and then repeating the step—hundreds, if not thousands, of times for each moccasin.

My grandma Annie Two Hawk did the same with belts and leather bags. But her specialty was prayer-book covers.

As I have described before, both of them faced their share of hardship and difficulty. Yet, for me, the persistent and quiet manner in which they did beadwork is among the enduring memories I have of each of them. Each of them produced beautiful work, and many pieces are now family heirlooms. So is their persistence. With the quiet, steadfast, and unhurried manner with which they approached their tasks, they showed me how I should live my life. They showed me how to be resilient.

All of my grandparents epitomized the best qualities and characteristics of being human, among them resiliency. They faced the worst that life threw at them with the best of what they were. Just as important, they demonstrated one significant reality about resiliency: it is a quiet, persistent process. While hardship, difficulties, and disaster might befall us in a blinding moment, resiliency responds subtly. It does not bring results in one fell swoop, but moment by moment and one step at a time.

My maternal grandparents and I eventually moved from our house on the plateau into town. The horses and the wagon were sold, and we rented a small house in town. From that moment on, I encountered new and strange realities, such as having neighbors thirty yards away, rather than three miles. Over time, we adjusted, more or less, to life in town. Our mode of transportation was gone, so we walked. Walking was nothing new, but now it was our only way to get anywhere.

In town, we were five miles from church. That was no reason not to go, especially in good weather. At the time, my grandmother was fifty-five, and my grandfather was sixty-seven. On Sunday mornings we arose early, got dressed, ate a hearty breakfast, and headed south on foot. We started early so that if we had to walk the entire five miles, we would still arrive in time. More often than not, however, we managed to catch a ride. Some other member of the congregation or someone who happened to be driving in the same direction would give us a lift. Getting a ride home was never a problem.

I do not remember exactly how many times we walked all the way to church—perhaps about a dozen. As a boy full of energy, I did not regard that time and having to walk as a hardship. It was just one of the ways my grandparents and I did things. When, as an adult, I look back on that time, I realize that my grandparents could have stayed home and bemoaned the fact that there was no way to get to church. Instead, they adjusted to the situation with one simple thing: resiliency. We faced the situation and got to church, one step at a time.

Bad times may swoop in in one awful moment. Difficulty and hardship may take us by surprise and then take us down a long and painful path. But trouble does end, one way or another, and if we are fortunate enough to stand back up and dust ourselves off, then we go on. We go on by relying on the qualities and aspects of our character that are just as powerful as whatever brought the hardship. Even if you think you do not have those qualities and the kind of character it takes, someone else has them and has shown you how it is done. The examples are all around, sometimes closer than you might think.

As all of my grandparents said and showed in one way or another, when life throws its worst at you, face it with the best you have.

There is no other way to live life.

6

The Stone Carriers

In a time long ago, two travelers were walking across
a wide, grassy plain. They were on a quest to the great
mountains farther to the west. In a vision, a seer from
their village had seen a mountainside of shiny black stone,
a kind of stone that had been born of fire, she was told
by the spirits. This stone could be fashioned by a skilled
artisan into knife blades and points for lances and arrows.
Blades and points made of that black stone would be
sharper and, therefore, more lethal.

The two men reached the very edge of the plains,
farther than either of them had ever traveled west. For that
matter, no one among their people had gone as far. The
elders had selected them, knowing they had the courage
to go into the unknown, because there was more at stake
than shiny stones.

For several years, the people had been at peace. Some
of the young men were restless, anxious for excitement,
but many were complacent. Though hunting was
necessary to feed their families, many questioned the need
for the warrior. They felt the people did not need every

man to be a fighting man, the protector. For many years, the elders had talked about what to do. One day, Shell, the old seer, had a vision, an answer to their predicament. All they needed were two good men.

The elders had chosen Grass and Yellow Bow for their determination. Neither had ever shirked their responsibilities. Their sense of duty, the elders knew, would be put to the test. After all, they were sending the men into unknown territory and on a quest their people had never attempted. Furthermore, the journey would be fraught with known and unknown dangers and enemies.

Grass was the older of the two, a widower. As a young man, he had seen battle against his people's enemies, and he was a deliberate and thoughtful man. Yellow Bow was younger and not yet married. He was physically strong and still young enough to approach things with a reckless courage.

They equipped themselves for their long journey, finding a balance between what they absolutely needed and what they could comfortably carry. Each of them carried two encased bows; a quiver of arrows; a short lance; a long, braided leather cord; a water bag; a food bag; spare moccasins; and two tanned deer hides, sewn together, to double as a coat and a sleeping robe. Each also had a knife and a fire starter. Anything else they could find or make.

An initial sense of excitement and bravado stayed with them the first two or three days. Eventually, however, the journey settled into monotonous routine. Awake at dawn, walk, stay alert and watchful for danger, rest occasionally, and make camp before sunset. Yellow Bow was the first to wear out the soles of his moccasins, after nearly fifteen days. It was a sign, it seemed, of the enormity of their task, and perhaps of hardships yet to come.

The landscape changed the farther west they went. The low, rolling hills and grassy prairies of their homelands became rocky buttes, with sparse grass and other plants they had never seen before. To the west, a seemingly endless line of mountains with high, jagged, and snow-covered peaks loomed on the horizon, stretching from south to north. According to the seer's directions, they were to cross over the first range of mountains and into a broad, dry valley. The mountain of black stone was somewhere in a second range of mountains. But in her vision, the seer had also seen a strange land—a land where the ground boiled like water. The shiny black stone was near there, she said.

Grass had taken that information in stride. The seer was old and wise, and her visions of the future were not to be taken lightly. She had never been wrong. Yellow Bow admitted to his companion that boiling land was hard to believe, no matter who said it.

Any further talk about such strange things was interrupted one day by a large bear, reddish brown in color, the kind with the hump between his shoulders. Grass and Yellow Bow were forced to make a wide berth north to avoid it. They noticed, however, that it had scented their tracks and was following them. To confuse the bear, they split up for half a day. At sundown, they met on a rocky hilltop they had spotted in the distance. Soon after that, they found a creek and walked in it to eliminate their scent. They did not stop until well into the night, and their tactic was successful.

But a bear was a small worry compared to the mountain range that stood before them. From a distance, its foothills and slopes were dark and foreboding. Yet the snow-covered peaks shined brightly in the sun. The seer had told them to find the highest peak with clouds around it. She said it would resemble an old man with white hair blowing in the wind. She was right—after another day's travel, they saw such a peak.

Grass decided that they needed to rest and replenish their food. They found a tree-choked bowl atop a hill and stopped there. The trees were scrub pine and short, stunted by the wind that seemed to blow often here. But the hilltop offered a wide view of the surrounding landscape. There they kept watch while they repaired their moccasins. On the second day, Yellow Bow spotted an elk and went after it. By evening, he returned with a hindquarter over his shoulder. At the next dawn, he and Grass went back to where he had hung the large pieces of the butchered carcass as far as he could up in a tree. That night they feasted well, eating better than they had for nearly a month.

In the daylight, the mountain range to the west filled the entire horizon. Neither Grass nor Yellow Bow had ever seen such high mountains. As the sun went down behind them, the mountains turned into a long, jagged shadow.

"How long do you think it will take us to cross them?" Yellow Bow wondered.

"Hard to know," Grass replied, sensing the younger man's apprehension. He knew it would never be expressed, but it was there. For that matter, Grass had been wondering how difficult it would be to get over those mountains.

"It is still the middle of summer," he said. "There is time. When we get to those eastern slopes, we will know what the land is like. Then we might know how long it will take to climb up and over the mountains."

That made sense to Yellow Bow. With their food bags full of elk jerky, they resumed their trek the next dawn.

Four days later, they came to the foothills of the great mountains. They did not know what to call them because no one among their people had ever seen them before— except for the seer, in her vision. She did say that, in her vision, the peaks shined in the sunlight. So Grass decided to call them the Mountains That Shine.

There was much game in the foothills and on the slopes. Elk were everywhere, and black tail deer. The first evening, Yellow Bow saw a goat with large horns curling backward. He also saw the footprints of several people. For three days, they climbed up the slopes, staying down in the gullies, off the crests of ridges. Each night they made camp without a fire. After two more days, they found a narrow pass. It was one of the strange goats with the curling horns that showed them the way over the mountain.

Once through the pass, they saw that it was a broad range of mountains, with more ridges to the west. The tall, cloud-covered peak stood like a white-haired giant to the south. Staying out of sight was not difficult because of the forested slopes. They had never seen such forests before; the trees seemed to go and on. It was easy to remain concealed and travel fast.

Though they could not travel in a straight line, they eventually reached the edge of the forest and then descended into another broad valley. The next range of mountains poked up like a line of dark clouds just over the horizon. That night, they made camp in a small overhang in a creek bed and built a fire.

"What if we cannot find the mountain of black stone?" Yellow Bow asked as he watched a rabbit roasting over the flames. He had killed it with one shot from his bow and had even managed to recover his arrow. Recovering arrows was a common practice, whenever possible, because arrows were difficult to make. "Can we be certain there is such a place?"

"There are many strange things in the world," Grass replied. "When I was a boy, I heard stories of little people."

"Little people? What do you mean?" the younger man scoffed.

"Little people. Not children. Grown people, but small. My uncle went east as a young man, to the Muddy River. In a village there he met the girl he would take as his wife. One day when he was hunting with some men, they took him to a place where the little people lived. When I was younger, he took me there. We waited near a hill, all day. We saw them. Little people, dressed like us and with hair down to the ground."

"You saw them?"

"I saw little people. So when the seer says there is a mountain of black stone, I believe her. To find it, among all those mountains over there, will not be easy. But we will try. Besides, we told the elders we would try, did we not?"

Yellow Bow nodded slowly. "I have never traveled this far in any direction from home," he admitted. "That alone is something."

"It is," Grass agreed. "Our villages would not be on the prairies if our grandparents had not been willing to go beyond the farthest place they had been and crossed the Muddy River. That is what life is. To take a risk and go past that farthest place. Besides, think what will happen when we return with shiny black stones," Grass said. "They will make us tell stories of our journey until we are old and gray."

Grass pointed west toward the next range of dark mountains that waited for them. "That is how far we will go, you and me. When some children hear our story, a few of them will look toward the setting sun, and they will wonder what is beyond how far we went."

Staying below the ridgelines and using the cover of creek and river bottoms as much as possible, they crossed the broad valley. After six days, they were once again on forested slopes. Along the way, however, they endured rainstorms that forced them to seek shelter. When it was not raining, the wind was steady.

Maintaining a northwesterly course, they made slow, but steady progress through the forests. More than once they had to avoid bears. Though they had seen old human footprints in the valley, they saw no sign of people in the mountains. On the third day, they came to a large lake with very cold water and saw fish with bright and colorful scales, a kind they had never seen. Fashioning spears, they were able to take two large ones. Searching and scouting carefully, they selected a narrow gully to cook their catch. The meat was very flavorful.

Grass thought they should find a good hidden shelter and rest for two days. After that, he wanted to scout each of the prominent ridges that surrounded the lake, just to see what they would see. Yellow Bow was not sure, but he trusted the older man's judgment. It was not until they circled to the west of the lake that they saw something hard to believe.

Water erupted out of the ground in a plume, shooting up into the air higher than the tallest trees nearby. It did so repeatedly, even after the sun went down. They could hear it hissing and splash back down to the bare earth. Almost as strange was the absence of animals. None, not even birds, came close.

They climbed high into a tall pine to watch the astounding sight. Yellow Bow was now less skeptical about the seer's vision. This was not the ground boiling, but it was the strangest thing he had ever seen in his life. He was afraid to think what kind of power made such a thing happen.

"How does it happen?" he asked Grass.

"I do not know," Grass replied. "There is a power here that I will never understand, and it is to be respected. There is a reason there are no animals here. They respect it, so we should not stay. Our purpose is to find the black stone. I know it is here somewhere."

Farther west of the erupting water, they found the very thing the seer told them she had seen. The earth itself was boiling. Mud in a pool bubbled up and popped. It was light in color, a very light brown. But even more astonishing was a pool of water. Grass was curious because he saw no fish or the usual insects that swam on the surface of still ponds. The water was also very clear. When he held his palm down to it, the water was hot.

They climbed to the crest of a bare hill to survey the immediate landscape. The bubbling earth was all around, as well as the clear pools of hot water. It was almost too hard to believe. There was one thing that was certain. Somewhere, perhaps nearby, was a mountain of shiny, black stone. The old seer had seen it in her vision, just as she had seen the boiling earth.

"How can this be?" Yellow Bow asked under his breath. "I never thought I would see something like this."

"This is a place of power," Grass replied. "If we stayed here long enough, we might understand it. But that is not the reason we are here."

They went away from the place of boiling mud and made camp in a thick grove of pine and aspen. It was cool among the trees as the sun went down. Taking a chance that no other people were nearby, they built a fire. Not only did it chase away the chill, but it was also reassuring and familiar. Not only had they traveled farther than any of their people ever had, but they had also seen things that were very hard to believe.

"There are many peaks and ridges," Yellow Bow pointed out, "all around us. Where do we start looking?"

"Wherever we want. I think we should begin to the west and circle to the north, then to the east," Grass suggested.

"I think we should keep our bows strung," Yellow Bow said. "And carry an arrow in the hand."

Grass nodded in agreement. Carrying an "arrow in the hand" meant to hold one arrow in the hand that held the bow. Holding an arrow that way, a good bowman could place it on the string and shoot in less than a heartbeat.

"I think we should be ready for anything," the younger man went on. "This is good country, pleasing to the eye, but the trees make it difficult to see far. That makes me uneasy. Anything can hide anywhere, just as we have."

"Yes," Grass said, "I have been thinking that there have to be people who live in these mountains. If so, they would know about this place and the shiny black stone. If they saw us, they would think of us as enemies. You are right. We have to be ready for anything."

They took time to inspect their weapons and then picked out landmarks to keep in mind. On a whim, Grass picked gray leaves from a low-growing shrub. When he rolled the leaves between his palms, they emitted a sweet scent. It seemed to be a kind of a sage. They picked more and rubbed themselves to cover their human scent, if nothing else to confuse bears. Then they began their search for the mountain of black stone.

Three hard days later, they made camp northwest of the deep lake. They saw a bear and several black-tailed deer and elk but found no mountain of black stone.

Their shelter was an east-facing overhang of rock, a crevasse that went back into the side of a ridge. A swatch of black smoke on the roof of the overhang was a telltale sign that someone had camped there before. They took turns keeping watch that night. As good as the shelter was, they decided not to return to it. It was a known place to someone, and sooner or later that someone would return.

They built their next shelter, giving in to the persistence of a steady drizzle that went on for two days. It forced them to make a shelter of leafy branches over a narrow gully. But they managed to make the shelter resemble a pile of driftwood, something that might have occurred naturally. In spite of the rain, ravens cawed and cackled frequently the day long, and at night wolves and coyotes howled. And mosquitoes were a bother all the time. A chorus of other animal voices could be heard, some occasionally and some frequently, such as the whistle of a bull elk.

When the skies cleared, they were glad to be moving again. They replenished their meat supply with several rabbits and a kind of grouse. Smaller game was easier and quicker to take. A deer or an elk usually ran great distances with an arrow impaled in it, and it was often hard to find the animal after it had expired.

By now they were well northwest of the deep, cold lake and had searched every ridge and butte around. They were tired of climbing up and down rocky slopes. Moccasins had to be repaired every evening. Home was only a memory now, and summer was waning.

Yellow Bow was worried about the weather in this unfamiliar place. "How much longer will we look for the black stone?" he asked. "Perhaps winter comes early here."

"We must assume that it does," Grass told him. "I think if we have not found the black stone by the time leaves start turning, we should go home."

So the seekers agreed. The sun's path across the sky was lower than it had been when they had started their journey, which meant that autumn was near. They sensed that winter in this land could be as harsh as it was in their home territory. More than that, it probably stayed long. Neither wanted to spend an entire winter away from home and family.

The situation took a good turn the next day. Yellow Bow saw fresh human tracks. Several people had crossed a narrow stream, leaving prints in the soft mud. Grass was especially intrigued because the tracks went both ways. The tracks going north covered those going south. Whoever made them had come and gone, and very recently. They decided to follow the prints south.

Through gullies and forest the tracks led them. Whoever the travelers were, they had been careful to stay out of sight. Which meant they were being cautious.

Near sundown Grass and Yellow Bow found themselves on a rocky, northwest slope. The prints had led to that area, but on the rocky surface, there were no signs. Taking advantage of the remaining daylight, they found a blown-down tree and made camp beneath the large tangle of exposed roots. It was a natural shelter that hid a small fire.

As the rays of the sinking sun sliced through the trees, Yellow Bow's sharp eyes saw reflections near the top of the slope. Something was glistening, not unlike sunlight on water.

"Look!" he called to Grass. "What is that?"

Their curiosity led them up the slope, both of them running, hurrying before the sun went down and left the slope in shadow. The pinpoints of light were coming from the surface of a bare vertical wall of rock—a smooth, shiny surface.

Panting from the climb, they stood for several long moments, staring at the shiny, dark wall of rock.

"Grandmother Shell was right," Yellow Bow said reverently. "This is the smoothest stone I have ever seen." He gently caressed a protruding ledge.

"Tomorrow we chip away pieces we can carry," said Grass. "Tonight we pray and give thanks."

Sleep was nearly impossible that night. Against all odds, they had found the shiny, black stone. Yellow Bow had picked up small pieces that had been left at the base of the wall. Their edges were sharp, easily slicing through the soft leather fringe on his shirtsleeve.

With the base of an elk-antler tine, Grass chipped away pieces of the black stone the next morning. He worked quickly, worried that someone might arrive at any moment. He managed to crack off four pieces, all about the size of his fist. They noticed that the stone was indeed dark, but some of it was reddish brown and some black. Light shone through the thinner flakes they found at the bottom of the vertical wall.

Grass left a small bundle of red willow tobacco at the base of the wall, as an offering for the stone they had taken from the mountain. They departed, almost reluctant to leave. By midday, they were far from the mountain with the shiny stone. They stopped, but only briefly, for a last look at the boiling mud. From a distance, they saw the plume of white water erupting over the tops of distant trees. These were sights they would not forget for the rest of their lives.

Knowing there were likely no people in this area, they shot an elk to replenish their food. They followed it for the rest of the day and found it at the bottom of a hill. They could take only one hindquarter and a small side of ribs. But they did take the hide. The wolves, whose tracks were everywhere, would find the rest of the carcass. That night, the men roasted the ribs and ate until they were uncomfortably full. The next day, they made jerky from the meat of the hindquarter and carefully inspected their weapons, making repairs where necessary.

Grass knew they had been exceedingly fortunate. Though they were footsore and a bit ragged, they had suffered no major injuries and had not fallen ill. How long their good fortune would hold was anybody's guess. Their only mission now was to make it home. Autumn had come to the high country. Yellow Bow pointed out the aspen and birch leaves that were starting to turn yellow here and there. Three days later, they reached the end of the east-facing foothills, just as a light snow fell.

That first snow did not last, but it forced them to wait until late afternoon, after it had melted, to move again. They did not want to leave tracks. Until sundown, they followed as many dry creek beds as possible to minimize any sign of their passing. Nights were getting cold, but they avoided making fires. In the open country, even a small, uncovered fire could be seen from great distances.

They retraced their path across the Mountains That Shine, staying north of the cloud-covered peak. The prairie they descended to was a welcome sight. A day east of the foothills of the mountains, they stopped to rest, to make new moccasins, and to work on their elk hide. Grass was looking for mint along a narrow creek. The enticing scent was drifting on the breeze, so he kept following it. Yellow Bow's attention was on his task of scraping the inside of the elk hide with his knife. He did not sense any danger until he heard a soft "woof."

A large, dark shape loomed in his vision as he turned to look, hitting him hard and knocking him backward.

Instinctively, the young man slashed out with his knife—a reaction that helped save his life.

The wolverine's teeth had torn open the point of his left shoulder, but Yellow Bow's knife had done damage as well. It sliced through the animal's neck at the base of the shoulder, cutting into a large vein—not that it slowed down the animal. Wolverines were feared by human and beast for two reasons: they were mean-spirited, and the only way to defeat one was to kill it.

Blood spurting from its neck, the dark-brown wolverine attacked again. Yellow Bow ducked and rolled, as his attacker's momentum carried him past. But it whirled in an instant, even as it was dying. Without looking, Yellow Bow knew his bow and arrows and lance were too far away to be of any use to him. He stumbled to his feet to meet the next attack he knew was coming. He ignored the excruciating pain in his shoulder and the blood running down his arm.

With a sense of detachment, he saw an arrow appear in the wolverine's side, then another in the next instant. The snarling wolverine turned toward his assailant, gathering himself to leap. Instead, its legs trembled, and the animal crumpled to the ground. Grass appeared, lance in hand, and stabbed the still-growling wolverine through the heart. In another moment, it was silent.

By sundown, Grass had managed to make a covered camp against a bank in the dry watercourse, as far away from the dead wolverine as possible. He managed to dig into the side of the bank and used the elk hide as a makeshift cover. On it he piled brush.

Yellow Bow's shoulder wound was long and deep. Grass cleaned it as well as he could, but he had seen wounds fester, especially from the bite of an animal.

"Thank you for saving my life, Uncle," Yellow Bow said, using the title of respect for a man not old enough to be a grandfather. "I did not see that thing until it attacked me."

"I am glad I was on my way back to camp," Grass said. "And fortunately it was a big and easy target."

"I can travel tomorrow," the younger man said gamely. "We need to stay ahead of the cold weather."

Grass shook his head. "I have a small bundle of red willow bark," he said. "Tonight I will make a poultice and put it on the wound. If that keeps it from festering, then we will travel."

A throbbing pain prevented Yellow Bow from sleeping. In the morning light, Grass saw that the poultice had not worked well enough. Around the wound were telltale red marks. There had not been, Grass guessed, enough red willow to draw out all the impurities from the wound. Furthermore, the younger man's face was hot to the touch. A fever so soon after a wound suffered was not a good sign.

"My friend," Grass said. "Here is what must happen. I must find more red willow. This is not our country, so I do not know exactly where to find it, except to look along a river bigger than the creek back there. It will take me a while."

Yellow Bow smiled wanly. "I will wait."

"I will pile brush on the shelter to hide it," Grass reassured his wounded companion. "You can cover yourself with my robe as well, so you will not need a fire. Keep your lance close."

Reluctantly, Grass left after doing all he could to hide the shelter. It did resemble a large pile of brush. With a last look back, he went around a bend in the dry creek and headed north. He remembered a creek that ran out of the foothills, and he was certain they were south of it. Grass settled into an easy trot. In one hand was his strung bow and an arrow. In the other was his lance. He had nothing else but a water bag, his knife, and coil of rope.

Grass stopped often to look back at the way he had come. He wanted to remember so he could find his way back to Yellow Bow in the dark, if he had to. The sun was sliding into the western half of the sky when he found a creek—a cold, fast creek. Upstream, it came from a thick forest, but he turned downstream. He was more likely to find any kind of short growth, like willow, in the open. The endurance of his youth was long gone, but he still kept a steady trot. His persistence was finally rewarded late in the afternoon. He found a stand of red willow along the creek.

Ordinarily, he would take his time and peel the bark, but the sooner he returned to the shelter, the sooner he could treat Yellow Bow's wound with new poultice. So he cut down several stalks and bound them together. He would peel them back at camp. After looking around to be certain no one or nothing was nearby, he started back.

Dusk caught him on the trail. He startled a young coyote and heard it scurry into the brush. From distant hills he heard a wolf, then another. Perhaps they were talking about him, he thought. Grass had to stop more frequently to catch his breath and rest. Fortunately, he recognized a sandstone formation and turned south. The moon came up and showed him the dry creek bed.

Yellow Bow was awake and relieved to see his companion. Grass worked quickly to strip the outer bark; it was the inner layer he needed. When he finished, there was a large pile of red bark. He hoped it was enough. Now he needed hot water. That meant a fire.

"I will make a fire," he said to Yellow Bow. "The shelter is well covered."

"Wait until daylight," the younger man said.

"No. Your wound has festered more. I must pull out the poison now, or it will be too late."

Grass had stopped to gather a handful of small stones, knowing he would have to boil water. There was plenty of fuel. After the fire was burning, he took his buffalo-horn cup from his arrow quiver. When the bed of coals was glowing beneath the flames, he put the stones on top.

Yellow Bow watched, his mouth set tight against the pain. Smoke, little though it was from the dry wood, stung his eyes.

In a while, the small stones were glowing. Before they cracked, Grass picked them up with a forked stick and dropped them into the water in the buffalo-horn cup. When he decided the water was warm enough, he stuffed as much red willow bark into the cup as he could.

He bound the poultice to Yellow Bow's shoulder. After that, he fell asleep.

Morning came cold and gray. As soon as there was light, Grass looked at the wound. Much of the angry red swelling had gone down. He prepared another poultice, and by midday, Yellow Bow said the pain was subsiding.

Low clouds stayed for two days, spouting a few snowflakes. Grass improved the shelter and built a small fire. They let it go out at dusk, but the coals lasted through part of the night. It was enough to keep the chill at bay, though it was not close to being warm. Grass used the last batch of red willow for one more poultice. Yellow Bow was restless, anxious to be going home. While Grass kept watch from a nearby rise in the afternoon, Yellow Bow sat outside the shelter.

That night, snug in the shelter, they talked.

"What have we proven?" Yellow Bow asked. "We went to a different country, walked for over sixty days. For what? Pieces of shiny stone that an old woman saw in a dream?"

Grass was surprised by the younger man's frustration, perhaps due to his encounter with the wolverine. "The elders asked, and we both agreed," he reminded his companion. "I probably will never do anything as difficult ever again. It was not easy, but I am glad for this journey."

"We are still a long way from home," Yellow Bow cautioned. "It took us thirty days to get this far."

"How you look at this journey is your choice," Grass said gently. "For me, it has changed the way I look at my life. It has taught me that I am stronger and more resilient than I thought I was. I have traveled farther than I ever thought I would. If you think about it, perhaps you will feel the same. Perhaps we have proven that everyone is capable of going farther than they think they can."

"You saved my life. I will never forget that," Yellow Bow assured Grass. "And I will never forget the water flying out of the ground, or the boiling mud. We were the first of our people to see those things."

"Those strange and wonderful things, those mysterious things, will always be part of your life," Grass pointed out. "No one can take that away."

After two more days of rest, Yellow Bow was no longer pale, and Grass decided he was strong enough to travel. His left arm was useless, however, because of the torn shoulder. Grass made a sling for it to keep it in place so the wound would not bleed. In spite of the discomfort, Yellow Bow stubbornly insisted on carrying his share of the load. Under a bright sky, they left the snug shelter and turned their footsteps east, toward home.

On the outbound journey, they had avoided the Black Mountains that stood at the western edge of their territory.

Going through them would have slowed them down, and they decided to skirt south of them for the same reason. But seeing them in the distance meant they were home.

The Black Mountains were named thus because, from a distance, their pine-covered slopes looked black. It was a holy place for the people, one that another seer long ago had seen in a vision.

East of the Black Mountains, after four months of hardship, monotony, and excitement, the journey nearly ended tragically. It might have, except for a single arrow.

Craving fresh meat, Grass and Yellow Bow had decided to rest for a day and set snares, hoping to trap rabbits. Late in the afternoon, they were checking the snares, Grass in one direction, Yellow Bow in the other. In one of the snares was a rabbit. Grass retrieved it and his snare and followed the creek bed back to camp. Around a bend, he came face-to-face with a black bear, a mere ten paces away.

Black bears are smaller than brown bears, but no less ferocious. This was a young male, powerful and in its prime. It rose on its back legs and stood taller than Grass. Assuming the bear had smelled the fresh rabbit carcass, Grass cautiously tossed it on the ground in front of the standing bear. The bear was not interested. Its small, dark eyes stayed on Grass.

There was no place to run—the nearest tree was too far. Besides, bears are faster than humans. Grass had not strung his bow and had gone away from camp without his lance. He knew that any sign of retreat, like a step backward, would likely prompt the bear to attack. Grass waited, hoping the bear would lose interest and walk away.

But it was not to be. The bear dropped to all fours and moved slowly toward Grass, a sure sign it would attack. Another sign was that it had not taken its gaze away from Grass. At four paces, it paused, its black nose quivering as it took in the odors and scents all around. Then the bear became absolutely motionless. Grass reached for his knife, deciding he would not go down without a fight.

He heard a slight hiss, a familiar sound, an instant before the bear let out a bellow of rage and pain and leaped off the ground. Grass instinctively jumped out of the way, then felt a hand on his arm. It was Yellow Bow.

They moved away and ducked behind a clump of soapweed to watch. The bear was slashing at its own face; at the same time, it was spinning and staggering. It fell and jumped up again, resuming its crazy dance and howling its rage. Grass was puzzled for a moment, then he saw what had saved his life.

An arrow was protruding from the bear's head, through the eye sockets, in one and out the other. Yellow Bow's arrow had blinded the bear and was driving it mad. But Yellow Bow had paid a price for his astonishing shot. The wound on his left shoulder was bleeding.

Quickly gathering clumps of gray prairie sage, which grew in abundance, Grass twisted it into a large bundle and bound it tightly to the wound. The bear's squeals and howls did not subside, and it shredded its own face trying to dislodge the cause of the pain. It had ceased its dance and stood on all fours, shaking its head from side to side.

"We have to put it down," Grass said.

"Get close," Yellow Bow advised. "Close enough to put an arrow in its heart."

Thus, Grass put the bear out of its misery.

Ten days later, they found their village. The people had moved in preparation for the autumn hunts, relocating to a small valley full of giant cottonwood trees. Everyone was astonished to see the two travelers alive.

Some of the story of their journey did not have to be told in words. It was there for everyone to see: Yellow

Bow's wound; a new kind of mountain sage that Grass had picked; their tattered and ragged clothing, gaunt faces, and thin bodies; a fresh bear skin and its skull with an arrow through the eye sockets; and, of course, four shiny, black stones.

As Grass had predicted, they had to tell their story over and over again. Shell, the old seer and medicine woman, healed Yellow Bow's wound. Grass gave her the sage he had picked in the mountains.

After two bison were taken in the first autumn hunts, the people feasted and honored the two travelers. They had been gone for nearly a hundred days.

A special container was made for one of the stones, and it was placed in the council lodge for everyone to see and touch. From the other three, the elders directed that lance points and arrowheads were to be made. The most skilled point makers set to work. Two special lances were made, tipped with the black stone and decorated, and given to Grass and Yellow Bow. Other lance points and arrowheads were distributed among the hunters. One arrow tipped with a black stone arrowhead became the symbol for a new warrior society—the Stone Carriers. Its first two members were Grass and Yellow Bow.

To join the Stone Carriers society, the requirement was simple and daunting: make the journey and return with the black stone. In two years, the elders announced, Grass and Yellow Bow would select two young men to make the journey, if there were any who were brave enough.

By the end of the next summer, a new lodge was made by the women for the Stone Carriers society. One of the first things placed in it was the tanned hide of a black bear, with an arrow through its eye sockets. On the hide hung a new arrow with a shiny, black-stone point.

Grass and Yellow Bow were the only men who had earned the right to sit in the lodge. The only others who entered it were the women who pitched it and took it down and cared for it—Grass's sister, Yellow Bow's mother, and their helpers. Not even the elders or Shell entered. Four years were to pass before the first new member was admitted. In time, others sat with Grass and Yellow Bow, but never more than eight at one time.

The first members of the Stone Carriers society were known just as much for their quiet ways as for their courage. They would remain lifelong friends, until Yellow Bow was killed while leading a war party and fighting, though badly outnumbered, against a tough enemy from the south. Grass's trek, at the age of nearly sixty, to recover his friend's body became almost as legendary as their journey to find the mountain of black stone.

Shell's vision had come to pass, but even she could not foresee what she had put in motion. Grass and Yellow Bow's journey did indeed inspire young men to seek the path of the warrior for the good of the people, as she and the elders had hoped. From that time on, every man answered the call to be the protector as well as the provider. Eventually, a new kind of warrior emerged, one who ventured alone into distant lands, often to the very lodge doors of the enemy—the scout.

As time went on, scouts carried on a strange little ritual, and over time its origin faded to the other side of memory. No one could remember how it had started. In the war bag, along with each man's special medicine objects, paints, and tools to repair weapons, every scout carried one other item—a small stone.

Afterword

Parting Shots

TRY AS I MIGHT, I can find nothing meaningful, beyond their obvious uses, in any of the gimmicks and gadgets at my beck and call. Computers, cell phones, and printers do not inspire me to think of my life and the kind of person I might be. Perhaps it is because I grew up in a time when technology was not an in-your-face part of life and was not regarded as the symbol of human achievement or superiority, at least among the people who mattered to me.

Decades ago, technology was not a god; using it was still somewhat of a choice. I knew of several families, mostly Indian and some white, in the late 1940s and early 1950s who were leery of electricity. Like the telephone, it was one of the new things in our part of the world, especially for Indians.

Without knowing exactly how it was produced artificially, Indians already had a word for electricity because they knew what it was. The word was *wakangli* (wah-khan-glee), which means "lightning." What fascinated and even awed many Indians was that white people had found a way to make lightning. They had somehow harnessed one of the great powers of the world.

Modern technology is obviously different from primitive technology. In some ways, modern technology seems self-sufficient, almost as if it does not need people. That is probably why many people over the age of sixty do not feel warm and fuzzy toward cell phones or computer monitors.

In 1960, my grandmother wanted to make a telephone call to my uncle, who lived in the eastern part of the state, on another reservation. We walked to the house of a local pastor who had a telephone. Those were the days before direct dialing, but with the assistance of the operator, we were able to place the call. When my uncle came on the line, he wanted to talk directly to my grandmother. She was hesitant, however, insisting that I pass on her message instead. Her apprehension over using the telephone was not because she did not understand how it worked. The Lakota word used to describe the telephone was *omasape* (oh-mahs-ah-pe), meaning "to strike the iron." This term referred to how the telegraph worked, where the key struck the copper plate.

My grandmother explained her reluctance to use the phone by saying, "My English is not so good." She assumed that she was not to speak Lakota over the telephone.

Today's technology cannot (and probably should not) be regarded as anything more than useful and entertaining gadgets, machinery, and instruments. Entertaining and useful is the sum total of what these things are. And it is a safe bet that most people do not know the raw materials their favorite piece of technology is made from nor how those materials were manufactured.

That cannot be said about a primitive bow and arrow. What they are is not a mystery to me, and neither are what they were made from nor how they were made. They are examples of some of the simplest forms of technology. Because of that, they remind me of two things: (1) that (for me at least) there was a time when life was simpler, and (2) that most things can be reduced to simple elements in order to understand them.

In order to understand the journey that is my life, I have chosen to look at it through the elements that are the topics for this book: transformation, simplicity, purpose, strength, and resiliency. The first is a process, a lifelong event, if you will, and the rest are characteristics acquired throughout life. I believe all are part of everyone's journey.

Transformation

Life is a process, which means that each of us is a work in progress. Everything we experience adds to what we are as a person. There was a time when two Lakota words had a hallowed meaning: *winuhcala* (wee-knew-hcah-la), meaning "old woman," and *wicahcala* (wee-chah-hcah-la), meaning "old man." These were titles of respect and meant that old women and old men were knowledgeable and wise and not just old in years. They had lived life, and in facing and enduring all manner of good and bad that a long life constitutes, they had been forged and transformed by it.

We cannot opt out of being transformed, but we should understand that there are two kinds of lessons: those that teach *how* and those that teach *how not* to be or to do.

Simplicity

A bow and an arrow will always remind me of simplicity and that a life without complications is what we all should strive for. All that we think we need we probably do not, and the less we are burdened by things or troubles, the easier it is to move.

I remember the story of a Lakota man, a hunter and a warrior, who in the old days had been captured by enemies. He found a way to escape, but he was dressed only in a breech-clout—no shirt, no leggings, no moccasins. He also had no weapons and no food.

In the months it took him to make his way home, he found or made the tools and weapons he needed to survive. With a deer antler, he fashioned a knife blade from stone (probably flint or chert). With the knife, he sliced strips of leather cord off his breechclout to use as an essential component of a bow-drill fire starter: the string. The other components were wood, which was plentiful. He collected stones to throw and was able to kill grouse and rabbits. With the knife blade, he also cut a hardwood limb to make a bow and thin stalks for arrows. With the rawhide from the skin of rabbits, he made a bowstring as well as a sling. He built shelters as he made his way home and kept himself warm at night with the fires he made. With his bow, he took deer, enough to have plenty of meat and hides from which to make clothing and moccasins.

His life, his very existence, was reduced to the simplest level, but he survived. Though the enemy had taken away everything he had, they could not take away what he knew or what he was.

PURPOSE

Purpose can coincide with a job or career, or it can be something apart from either. History tells us of people from Europe who became indentured servants in colonial America. They did so because it was the only way for them to obtain passage to the colonies. After they arrived, their contracts were sold to landowners. Overall, indentured servitude occurred because of a need for cheap labor in the colonies. After four to seven years of hard work, they were free. Some of them were given small plots of land, seeds, a cow, and new clothes. Indentured servitude was a means to an end. It was a way, as harsh and difficult as it was for most, for people to achieve their real purpose: to be free and to have the opportunity to build a life for themselves.

To know your purpose, to find it, and to honor it day in and day out is one of the secrets to life. Furthermore, I believe that any purpose that is selfless is the most fulfilling of all.

STRENGTH

In my earliest concrete memories of my grandparents, all of them were physically strong people. They were all active, worked hard, and had strong, calloused hands. The images of my grandmothers doing all manner of hard physical jobs—cultivating gardens, splitting wood, hanging out and taking down laundry, standing over a hot cooking stove, and shucking corn by the bushel—are as clear as though they happened only yesterday.

My maternal grandfather built a log house practically alone. My paternal grandfather was the taller of my two grandfathers and taller than most men. I have a photograph of him in his doughboy uniform, circa 1918; he was so young, yet so imposing at the same time.

I watched my grandparents age into their sixties, seventies, and eighties, and their physical stature diminished. It was a subtle transformation. Suddenly, there were new wrinkles on their faces and a slight stiffness in their movements. I know now, however, they were growing stronger in ways that mattered more: emotionally and spiritually. Their transformation culminated in the kind of strength they all had in abundance—wisdom. Their stature then, to me, was bigger than life—and still is.

RESILIENCY

I have been shooting the latest bow I made. This one is hickory, fifty-six inches long, and not quite a pound in actual weight.

But it probably pulls about fifty pounds at a twenty-two-inch draw. By now, it has fired a few thousand arrows. Every time I pull and release, the arrow flashes toward the target, and the limbs return to their original position, ready to send the next arrow. That is resiliency.

All of my grandparents had the same character. I was with my paternal grandmother, Blanche, in 1980 when one of my aunts and her husband brought news of the death of her oldest son, my uncle Narcisse. He had died of an accidental gunshot. My grandmother sat quietly, a handkerchief in her hands, which were folded in her lap as she listened. Then she wept quietly. After that, she comforted the rest of us. Her enormous strength of spirit carried her through a difficult time, and her resiliency enabled her to go on from there. She went back to being Grandma Blanche, ready to take on whatever else life sent her way, good and bad.

Bows and arrows, at least in their atavistic, primitive, and traditional forms, are of no consequence to most people in the world. But they still matter to some of us. They represent life and my journey through it. They will always remind me of the lessons I have learned in life, and they will always remind me of my grandparents.

I am especially blessed because of my grandparents, because of the kind of people they were, and because their lives and their character are examples for us—all the grandchildren who happened to be paying attention.

My maternal grandfather was the one who taught me about bows and arrows, how to make them and use them. Bows and arrows brought out his boyish side whenever he shot them, and I can feel his presence each time I walk out to my backyard with bow and arrows in hand.

The lessons I take from the bow and arrow are simple: life is the bow maker, and we are transformed by all the experiences we have, all the choices we make or are made for us, and even by those we do not make. There are many values, habits, and characteristics we learn throughout life, but among the most important are simplicity, purpose, strength, and resiliency.

It is time for me to string my bow and grab my arrows.

Acknowledgments

THIS BOOK IS my fourth project with Sounds True, and I am grateful that someone there thinks I have something worthwhile to say. That "someone" would include Tami Simon and Jennifer Y. Brown. *The Lakota Way of Strength and Courage* started as another topic under a different title several years ago. So thank you to Tami and Jennifer for their patience.

A special thank you to my editor, Amy Rost, for facing the trials and tribulations of a first-draft manuscript. It may be an adventure writing them, but I think it is quite another to wade through a first draft and make sense of it. I admire editors.

As ever, I must mention the elders of my childhood, beginning with all of my grandparents. They put me in touch not only with family history and legacy, but also with the past in general and many times very specifically. There were other elders as well, relatives and friends of my grandparents from the Rosebud and Pine Ridge Reservations. All of them were a glimpse into what Lakota people had been in the past and what we modern Lakota should strive to carry into the future. Furthermore, all of them were examples of strength and courage.

About the Author

JOSEPH M. MARSHALL III was born and grew up on the Rosebud Sioux Indian Reservation in South Dakota. Because he was raised in a traditional native household by his maternal grandparents, his first language is Lakota. In that environment he also learned the ancient tradition of oral storytelling. He is a specialist in wilderness survival and a practitioner of primitive Lakota archery, having learned from his grandfather the art of handcrafting bows and arrows.

Joseph writes full time and has published nine nonfiction works, three novels, a collection of short stories and essays, a children's book, and several screenplays. He has also appeared in several television documentaries, served as technical advisor for movies, and had a role in a major TV network movie, *Return to Lonesome Dove.* In 2005, he was a technical advisor and narrator for the six-part miniseries *Into the West,* in which he also acted the role of Loved By The Buffalo.

In 2000, Joseph became a Fellow in the Sundance Institute. He has traveled extensively across the United States and internationally as a speaker and lecturer. He developed a leadership seminar based on the lessons of the great warrior Crazy Horse, whose biography, *The Journey of Crazy Horse: A Lakota History,* he wrote primarily from oral accounts.

One of Joseph's most treasured and meaningful experiences was to be one of the founders of Sinte Gleska University (1971) on the Rosebud Sioux Indian Reservation. He is one of the Charter Board Members.

Joseph and his wife, Connie (also his literary agent and manager), are the parents of a blended family and have sixteen grandchildren.

For more information, please visit ThunderDreamers.com.

About Sounds True

SOUNDS TRUE is a multimedia publisher whose mission is to inspire and support personal transformation and spiritual awakening. Founded in 1985 and located in Boulder, Colorado, we work with many of the leading spiritual teachers, thinkers, healers, and visionary artists of our time. We strive with every title to preserve the essential "living wisdom" of the author or artist. It is our goal to create products that not only provide information to a reader or listener, but that also embody the quality of a wisdom transmission.

For those seeking genuine transformation, Sounds True is your trusted partner. At SoundsTrue.com you will find a wealth of free resources to support your journey, including exclusive weekly audio interviews, free downloads, interactive learning tools, and other special savings on all our titles.

To listen to a podcast interview with Sounds True publisher Tami Simon and author Joseph M. Marshall III, visit SoundsTrue.com/bonus/JosephMarshallLakota.

3/12